NO MORE MEETINGS!

Unlearn 'bored room' practices to change the way we connect

Mike Bonifer & Jessie Shternshus

No More Meetings!
by Mike Bonifer and Jessie Shternshus

For information, contact
BDI Publishers, Atlanta, Georgia,
bdipublishers@gmail.com.

Illustrations by Maya Shternshus
Cover Design: Tudor Maier

BDI Publishers

Atlanta, Georgia

ISBN: 978-1-946637-15-4
FIRST EDITION

It's time we put a stop to the epidemic of meetings! This is an issue of business health, and it's time we stop looking away from this threat to our well-being. But quitting is hard to do. You gotta prepare for withdrawal. Oh, and the cravings. "No More Meetings!" will give you what you need to stop your addiction and quit cold turkey.
— Clint Schaff, Vice President, *Los Angeles Times*

Mike and Jessie offer frames, games and inspiration to help teams embrace a disrupted status quo and reinvent how we connect, collaborate and transform in a diverse and dispersed workplace. #nomoremeetings
— Donna Pahel, Founder and CEO, 21 Day Story

Mike Bonifer and Jessie Shternshus have done it again! They have an amazing ability to look at everyday tasks and innovatively remake them. If your world is anything like mine you will appreciate the framework the authors have created to help move you and your team away from the seemingly endless low productivity meetings to engagements that are fun, creative, and time-effective. Buy this book!
— Jeff Roberts, Sustainable Energy Strategist

This book makes a big claim – no more meetings? Could this be possible? Not that we need less coming together in the workplace, but how often do we really meet the ideas, concerns, and creativities of others during the kinds of soul-sucking meetings well-known to anyone who picks up this book? What Bonifer and Shternshus have written is more than entertaining (though it is that). The practices they describe make minds sharp and relationships stronger. The book outlines clever ways to focus on common business processes – problem solving, consensus building, design thinking, etc. – with lively prose. It's clear that Mike and Jessie take games seriously, while assuring us we don't even need to call them that – no one ever has to know...

— Pamela M Buckle Ph.D.
Robert B. Willumstad School of Business
Adelphi University

Your organization's culture is embodied in the countless meetings you have every day, yet we rarely utilize these spaces to their full potential. This great, practical book uses the frame of games and improv to unlock the potential of these spaces for connection, productivity and imagination. This is a perfect sequel to Mike's first book: *GameChangers*!

— Andres Marquez-Lara
Founder and CEO, UFacilitate

Meetings are rituals at the workplace, and organizing meetings with intention and attention using the frames and games proposed in this book can make any manager or meeting facilitator a lot more effective. A timely book in the period of COVID to upgrade your online facilitation skills. Thank you Mike and Jessie!

— Abhinav Agarwal, Innovation Strategist

Meetings, meetings, everywhere,
the more we meet the less we care.

— Shternshus

Don't M with me
Anything but M with me
B with me
C with me
Even P with me or F with me
But please don't ask to M with me

— Bonifer

How To Eliminate All Meetings In One Move

Among the most-frequently heard complaints by employees, no matter how large or small their organization, or its reason for being, is that they get pulled into too many meetings.

That most meetings are too long. A slog.

That they involve too many people, many of whom don't need to be there in the first place, and spend most of the meeting distracted by texts, calls and emails anyway.

How do we get rid of these banes of our working lives? Improve our interactions? Avoid bringing along all our old meeting habits to our new virtualized WFH and WFA workplaces? We begin by *giving them another name!* If we never use the word meeting, we will have No More Meetings! Boom! Done! Gone! You're welcome.

For the rest of this book you will not see us use the word m***ing again. If we don't go there, we have lessened the odds that our day will be marred by them, and by all the work we're expected to do in the interstitials between one m***ing's over-ambitious agenda and the next one's narcotizing video gallery.

Okay, now that we've gotten that out of the way and eliminated all m***ngs from our daily schedule, what's going to take their place? We can't eliminate them from the calendar without creating a gigantic vacuum of unstructured time. Nature and management abhor vacuums. Activity will move into the vacuum, and if we don't do something about it, we can tell you what that activity is going to be: M***ings. M***ings with a vengeance. M***ings that have payback on their minds for what we tried to do with them, and will make themselves more painful than they've ever been before. Folks, if you thought they accomplished nothing before, revenge m***ings will hold you hostage to the point where you'll be paying ransom money to use the restroom.

We can't eliminate the need for people to gather, nor would we want to. Such gatherings are the basis of a group's culture and provide humanity and the bonding to create a shared sense of purpose in an enterprise. What we can do is make our work gatherings more meaningful, more human, more purposeful, more creative–maybe even more fun. What you'll get in our book are a bunch of ways to do just that. The same old processes won't resolve brand new problems.

Frames and Games

It's not enough to change what you name your gatherings. In order to affect their outcomes, you've got to change their structure, too. That's what we do in this book–change structures for your collaborations in order to improve your outcomes.

Each type of gathering described in our book has two components: a **Frame** and a **Game**.

The Frame describes the purpose and context of a gathering. Examples of Frames are 'Brainstorm a Campaign,' 'Plan an Event' and 'Team Building.'

A Game provides structure and process to a gathering along with the types of business outcomes a group can expect from it. Games have names like 'Quilting Bee,' 'Acid Test,' and 'Complaint Symphony.'

Frames are listed alphabetically in the book, with each Frame having a corresponding Game. Games are not solely tied to a Frame, you can adapt a Game structure for any purpose that suits your business objective, where the emphasis is on fast and effective collaborations.

Games are categorized so you can find one that suits your purpose. They have one or more of the following objectives, indicated for each entry:

Innovation
Communication
Collaboration
Customer Success
Strategy

Each Game has a suggested duration–though most Games can be played at different durations up to an entire day, or even two, if their activities are spaced that way. Some Games can be played asynchronously. These are indicated in the Table of Contents and throughout the book.

Many of the Games can be played in both physical space and online. Some are designed as online activities and can only be played that way. Others can only be played in physical space.

These designations, too, are in the Table of Contents and throughout the book.

For Games conducted online, we like Mural for whiteboards and sticky notes. Zoom, Google Docs/ Hangouts, Skype and Teams all have lots of users, and it's good to be conversant in multiple platforms, as customers and stakeholders may insist on a different platform for a collaboration. Of course many platforms support these functions. Sometimes these choices are made for us. If they're not, it's important that your group agrees on its communication platforms.

And this is important, too: You don't have to announce to your group that you're going to conduct your business by playing Games. Describe these interactions using language your group will know and understand. Then play away!

TABLE OF CONTENTS

FRAMES / GAMES

Each entry has one or more of the following objectives:
- Innovation
- Collaboration
- Communication
- Customer Success
- Strategy

The highlighted objectives will be covered in that FRAME/GAME

Positivity / Halos and Wings[#]

Page 127		Innov	Collab	Comm	Cust	Strat

Post Mortem / Dearly Departed[#]

Page 132		Innov	Collab	Comm	Cust	Strat

Presentation Prep / Pitchback[#]

Page 134		Innov	Collab	Comm	Cust	Strat

Prioritization / Tag Team Knockouts[#]

Page 137		Innov	Collab	Comm	Cust	Strat

Problem Solving / Sorry, Gong Number[#]

Page 141		Innov	Collab	Comm	Cust	Strat

Process Analysis / Acid Test[#+]

Page 144		Innov	Collab	Comm	Cust	Strat

Process Improvement / One Fail, Five Positives[#+]

Page 150		Innov	Collab	Comm	Cust	Strat

Professional Development / Each One Teach One[#]

Page 152		Innov	Collab	Comm	Cust	Strat

Ramping Up / Quilting Bee

Page 156		Innov	Collab	Comm	Cust	Strat

Re-framing a Challenge/ Re-express Yourself

Page 160		Innov	Collab	Comm	Cust	Strat

Re-framing a Challenge / What's Within Reach[##]

Page 162		Innov	Collab	Comm	Cust	Strat

Re-tooling / Medium Rare[+]

Page 165		Innov	Collab	Comm	Cust	Strat

Retrospective / Back to the Future[#]

Page 168		Innov	Collab	Comm	Cust	Strat

Retrospective / Mood-o-Meter[#+]

Page 174	Innov	Collab	Comm	Cust	Strat

Roadmapping / Mapper's Delight[#+]

Page 177	Innov	Collab	Comm	Cust	Strat

Social Idea Sharing / Light My Fire[#]

Page 180	Innov	Collab	Comm	Cust	Strat

Stand-up / Continue, Consider[#]

Page 183	Innov	Collab	Comm	Cust	Strat

Storytelling / Sign Safari

Page 186	Innov	Collab	Comm	Cust	Strat

Team Building/ Spirit Vegetable

Page 189	Innov	Collab	Comm	Cust	Strat

Trust Building/ Hide in Plain Sight

Page 193	Innov	Collab	Comm	Cust	Strat

Trust Building / Two Truths and a Lie[#]

Page 196	Innov	Collab	Comm	Cust	Strat

Unlearning / Fresh Take[#+]

Page 199	Innov	Collab	Comm	Cust	Strat

Urgency / Headline News[#]

Page 202	Innov	Collab	Comm	Cust	Strat

Visual Thinking / Huddle Pass[#+]

Page 205	Innov	Collab	Comm	Cust	Strat

[#]Denotes Game works in both physical and online environments

[##]Denotes Game designed specifically for online environments

[+]Denotes Game can be played asynchronously

FRAME: Active Listening

You call it eavesdropping.

"That's just creepy!" you say. "Who cares what people are talking about in the break room?"

"Where do you think stories come from?" we ask. "Great storytellers are great eavesdroppers. Eavesdropping is their thing. The listener isn't collecting evidence. She's using the eavesdropped conversations as inspiration for stories."

You say, "Well...you may have a point. About the *listening*."

"We're glad you're coming around," we say. "There are times and places for everything. If people talk loudly enough to be overheard, something in them wants to be heard, and we can listen without betraying anyone's relationships or violating their confidence."

"How?" you ask.

"This game," we say.

GAME: Eavesdrop

Active listening is an essential communication skill, and yet when do we ever get a chance to practice it? One of the crucial parts of active listening is engaging with your ears and eyes by reading an email while also being in a conversation. In the same conversation, we are listening to multiple conflicting points of view held by people trying to solve a problem. It can mean simultaneously reading emotions and literal language. Active listening, or as we're calling it for purposes of playing this Game, eavesdropping, means synthesizing these points of view into a whole. It means we create a coherent narrative in which all voices are heard and honored. This game will give you practice doing that.

People love listening to other people's conversations even if they don't want to admit it. So let's just all admit that we do it. Today we are going to give everyone permission to eavesdrop. You heard us right. Eavesdropping made okay!

- First, set up a circle of chairs, each two feet apart, in the middle of the room to accommodate everyone in your group (up to 20 people).

- Then give everyone an index card and a pen.

- Have people sit in each one of the chairs.

- Designate one person in the group to be the Eavesdropper: the BIG E!

- Ask the people in the chairs to pair up (or work in three if an odd number) and begin a conversation about something that's happened recently in their lives. It could be anything: a new pet at home, a birthday or milestone, a trip.

- With these conversations underway, the Eavesdropper is given two minutes to walk around the outside of the circle, in any direction, eavesdropping on conversations, and writing down words or phrases that catch their ears.

  The Eavesdropper can spend as much time as they want on any conversation but must listen to each conversation at least once. They can return to any conversation multiple times during their two-minute listening session.

  The Game's objective is for the Eavesdropper to put together a one-minute story from the words and phrases collected from overheard conversations.

- The story must be shared immediately with the full group and only use words or phrases on the

Eavesdropper's index card. Okay, we'll spot you some prepositions and conjunctions, but other than *that*, it's simply the collected words and phrases read to the group so that they make a story.

Got it? If not, eavesdrop on someone explaining it to someone else.

• Once the Eavesdropper has shared their story, pick a new Eavesdropper, and have people in the circle change places and start new conversations about different topics. Switch places in the room and start yer yappin'. Repeat.

This game can be easily adapted to a virtual environment by pairing people in separate meeting rooms and giving the designated Eavesdropper the ability to move between meeting rooms.

This is an excellent way to improve your listening skills, let go of the script in your head, and connect with what's going on in the room. Fun, eh?

OBJECTIVE: Collaboration, Communication

SUGGESTED DURATION: 2 hours

PHYSICAL AND ONLINE ENVIRONMENTS

FRAME: Award Ceremony

Award ceremony: A rite of passage or commemoration. An idiosyncratic ritual.

In organizations, we tend to focus on what is required to do a job, often at the expense of recognizing the impact of doing the job on those around us, our customers, and our world. This coming-together describes a ritual that will call out and honor the impact of our work - what each person in the group has contributed to the outcomes, and how their contributions have affected our organizations and us.

GAME: ImpAct Awards

Time to end the game that results in crappy outcomes that you have to spend time and effort not getting blamed for or sucked into. To hell with that. Let's play a new game!

This game keeps you, your group and your company on track to appreciate one another, and your customers. It will replace heads-down processes and their siloed points of view with a more holistic approach.

- The names of all attendees are placed in a hat. Each attendee draws a name out of the hat.

- People should think about the person whose name they've drawn, their impact on them personally, on the team, on your organization, and/or on your customers. Take 30 minutes to create a two-minute speech and a handmade ImpAct Award to give to the person. Use found objects. Do not go out and buy anything.

- One by one, people step to the front of the room and, without revealing the person's name, read their speech about the person whose name they've drawn. Be playful, exaggerate for effect, make a speech in the style of awards shows and banquets, but be complementary. *This is not a roast.*

- At the end of the speech, they will reveal who they're talking about and hand the person their handmade ImpAct award. Round of applause for the honoree, accompanied by the type of fanfare music that typically accompanies awards. Woot, woot!

Everyone is familiar with award ceremonies, so you'll be working from a well-known idiom. Speaking in and playing with the idiom will liberate participants to express truths and emotions that would not be so apparent if you asked them to be serious and literal.

OBJECTIVE: Collaboration, Communication

SUGGESTED DURATION: 1 hour

PHYSICAL AND ONLINE ENVIRONMENTS

FRAME: Being Present

It's hard to sit still all day in front of a screen. At home. Moving between meetings without ever getting out of our chairs. Heads get heavy when they're not swiveling and gawking. Eyeballs get weary when every image is 18 inches away. Ears get bored with every sound coming from your pods. Where bodies go (or don't), minds follow. The reverse is also true. Pretty soon, our minds and bodies are trying to dance without moving. If you've ever been a freshman at a school dance, you know what that's like. Awk-ward. All you want is to be somewhere else. What's missing is movement. To be present in the room – no matter what kind of space it is – *move* in the room. Here's a way to do that online.

GAME: In the Frame

This game won't take the place of that Pilates class you're missing, but it can give you a good burst of stretch-and-be-happy energy. Get ready for some online physical fun! It can be played standing, seated or a combination of the two.

It can be played by 3-20 people. They must all be on a single screen in gallery view. (The game will not work if you have more people than can fit on one screen.)

The focus of the Game is to have *only two people on camera at the same time*. Here's how to play it:

- After a quick hello and/or round of intros, everyone moves *off-screen*.

- At that point, anyone can choose to re-appear on camera at any time, then move back off-camera at any time, to always have only two people 'in the room' simultaneously.

  It will not come easy. Be patient with yourselves. Go slowly at first. Take your time. Have fun with your screw-ups. Enjoy that beat when there's no one on-screen, and then six people decide to jump in at the same time. Sense the rhythm of the group. Build a sense of giving and taking, and full participation by everyone in the group. Don't be that person who gets impatient and jumps in at every lull. And don't be that person who never jumps in at all. Play along. Make having exactly and only two people on-screen at the same time, the most important thing you can do. Because at that moment, if you're playing along, it will be.

  The team is not allowed to pre-plan or strategize ahead of time. Don't get in your heads. Trust your instincts in the moment about when to lead and when to drop out of view.

- As the game goes on, get quicker with it. See if your group can build tempo and intensity by spending shorter intervals on-screen and being quicker to dive out of view if there are too many people in the gallery. Be present by listening with your eyes.

To debrief, ask the group: What did you notice? How did you know when to jump into frame and when to jump out? What behaviors characterize the group's performance? What emotions came up?

Discuss how the group's observations relate to their current collaboration process. If these observations suggest ways to improve your collaborations, agree to begin putting them into practice regularly.

OBJECTIVE: Collaboration

SUGGESTED DURATION: 30 mins

ONLINE ENVIRONMENTS

FRAME: Breaking Patterns

Have you ever suffered from a bad case of "Hat Head"? It's when you put on a hat for an extended period, and after taking it off, your hair takes the shape of the hat, and you walk around all day looking like a character in a high school production of *Grease*. We don't want people to have the Hat Head Curse at work. The Hat Head Curse happens when a person's head is in the same place every day. They are stuck in the same, predictable patterns of thinking or operating for so long that they can't manage to see or do things differently. Here's a way to lift that Curse and break that cycle.

GAME: Hats Off

Each person should arrive at the m***ing wearing a favorite hat, or they can be provided with a hat from a thrift shop collection you've prepared. From Kentucky Derby chapeaux to Halloween hats, to your favorite team's ball cap, anything goes. Seasonal is good. Idiosyncratic is even better.

- The game begins with everyone removing their hats and having a stack of 20-30 blank index cards handed to them by the facilitator, who introduces themselves as The Mad Hatter.

- At the Mad Hatter's cue, people pair up with one another. Without making any references to names, each person writes a compliment, virtue, or other form of praise for the other person and places it in the other's hat. People go around doing this until they have paired up at least once with everyone else in the troupe.

At any time during this activity, the Mad Hatter can call out a 'Caplication' such as:

  - Draw a card from someone else's hat and put it in your own.
  - Draw a card from someone else's hat and put it in another person's hat.
  - Draw a card from your own hat and place it in someone else's.
  - Do the same as above, but with two cards.
  - Swap hats with someone.
  - Etc. etc. etc.

- Finally, each person gets their own hat back. Participants take turns pulling index cards from their hat and reading them aloud to the full group.

- This goes on until all the cards have been read or until the Mad Hatter concludes the game.

This game is an awesome way for a group to bond and recognize the Group Mind – that all of us, together, are stronger and more capable (and have many more virtues) than any of us do on our own. The group will be sharing compliments, virtues, and praises, not of themselves, but the group.

VARIATION: The instructions by the Mad Hatter can be adjusted to focus the game on a specific scenario. For example, it could be about generating ideas, troubleshooting, or defining roles and responsibilities. To focus the game on troubleshooting, people would replace compliments on the cards with pain points around a particular problem. When pain points are drawn from hats and read aloud, the group discusses how to resolve them, and defines a solution or a plan of action for each pain point drawn.

OBJECTIVE: Communication, Collaboration

DURATION: 1 hour

PHYSICAL ENVIRONMENTS

FRAME: Breakthrough

How many times has this happened to you? Your team has been assigned to come up with a breakthrough idea, a never-before-rendered solution to a sticky problem. Then you find yourself in the Dreaded Conference Room: no windows (offering you a panoramic view of beige nothingness), a conference table that sits between you and the other participants like a swamp full of alligators waiting to eat your energy, fluorescent lighting that sucks the Vitamin D directly out of your soul, and a ventilation system that recirculates air first breathed when the airlines allowed smoking on their planes.

The most interesting thing in the room is the 1980's carpet because of the amount of static electricity it can generate—one brush of your foot charges you with enough electricity to power a small town.

Sound familiar? Too familiar? Feeling boxed in? Being in a stuffy conference room doesn't exactly scream breakthroughs. Ironically, we continue to have unrealistic expectations for creative outcomes at m***ings where the room is drabber than the basement in a morgue.

GAME: Chalk Walk

Take your convocation to the streets! Grab a box of multi-colored sidewalk chalk and use the sidewalk or parking lot as your whiteboard. Use the space to share ideas and concerns, and to create something unique together.

- Weather permitting, get your chalk, and head outside.

- Pick a spot that can be observed from a window that looks down on the space, and where passersby will wonder WTF you're up to. One person in the group can be designated to stand in the window and photographically document the game's outcomes.

- Do a group drawing activity as a warm-up off to the side of where you'll be working. Using one piece of chalk, have each person in the group make one mark on the sidewalk, the only rule being you cannot lift the chalk. Take turns, with each person adding a mark to the drawing and connecting with the previous marks—not consciously trying to make a 'picture' but rather, connecting to see what picture emerges from the connections. Continue this until everyone has had three turns, or until a picture emerges, whichever happens first. Take a picture of your masterpiece to tape onto the refrigerator in the break room later.

- Draw two large 'whiteboard frames' and decorate them around the edges with designs like you'd see in a mosque, church, temple, or marijuana ad. This is sacramental work! One frame is for IDEAS, and the other is for QUESTIONS.

- Use the space to share ideas and concerns and create something unique and groundbreaking together.

Every suggestion must be made with a max of three words. Be succinct! Do not miss an opportunity to ask questions of passersby and get their input!

- Draw a third frame for keeper ideas. Here, as throughout the game, do a photo capture from the overhead window that can be saved for further processing and evaluation.

- Play a game of hopscotch to celebrate.

- Clean up your mess by pouring cans of LaCroix water over it. J/K. Pour Pellegrino.

Often, when we're working to resolve a problem creatively, we resort to the same framework we use for every other problem. That's not creative at all. To change the outcomes you're getting from your group, change the working environment. Replacing a 4'x8' whiteboard with a 400'x800' foot parking lot, and dry erase markers with sidewalk chalk is one way to do it.

OBJECTIVE: Collaboration, Communication, Innovation

SUGGESTED DURATION: 1-3 hours

PHYSICAL ENVIRONMENTS

FRAME: Building Consensus

Between all the cooking shows on television, and all the chili cook-offs that have tested digestive systems since the first chef added the first jalapeño to the first pot of beans, this is a format people know well. The format for this gathering is blind testing and voting on tactics to create consensus. Remove all identifying criteria as part of the research testing.

GAME: Stir the Pot

Make sure all participants know in advance what the group's primary objectives are for playing the game. Have all participants arrive with one to three ideas already written on 3"x5" index cards in black ink.

- You will have placed a piece of cookware large enough to hold the index cards (e.g. a pot or crockpot) on a table in the center of the room.

- When your *Stir the Pot* players arrive, have them place their cards into the cookware.

- The facilitator 'stirs the pot,' draws the index cards from the pot, and hands one to each person. All participants will have an index card in their hands that most likely isn't theirs.

- Have each person read the card to the rest of the group and then tape it to the wall. If people have put multiple cards in the pot, and there are more cards than people in the cook-off, continue drawing cards until all the cards have been drawn from the pot and taped to the wall.

- Once all the ideas are placed on the wall, have each person stand near an idea and read it to themselves. Give everyone a couple of minutes to read the idea and absorb it. Then have everyone rotate clockwise around the room looking at each idea for about three minutes until they make it back to the spot where they started.

- Hand out stickers depicting a hot food item such as a chili pepper. Each person gets three stickers.

- Ideas are voted on using dot voting and are ranked in order of 'hotness.' Hot (third-most stickers), Hotter (second most stickers), Hottest (most stickers). Go over the ideas that were ranked first, second and third, so that everyone knows where they landed as a team.

These ideas can be hung out in the hall or outside of the office doors, so everyone who didn't attend the m***ing can see the hot ideas.

The group will then need to decide on a roadmap to experiment with the final ideas or share it with their customers or internal partners.

OBJECTIVE: Collaboration, Innovation

DURATION: Half Day

PHYSICAL AND ONLINE ENVIRONMENTS

FRAME: Creative Ideation

As the renowned improv teacher, Dave Razowsky, says, "Repetition is not redundancy." This get-together involves repeating and re-stating ideas and problems until new meaning emerges. Actors of the Stella Adler School also use this technique.

GAME: Leapfrog

If your team is currently stuck on a problem or seems to use the same process for resolving every problem, no matter what it is, then maybe their brains need a bit of a jolt. A vigorous workout. This is a great activity to help people expand their way of thinking and doing, even when they have to work within constraints. It can be used as a warm-up for a longer session, or as a stand-alone session to prepare a team for an upcoming collaboration, such as an Agile sprint or production cycle.

- The facilitator begins the game by having everyone list everyday activities that can be demonstrated physically and 'read' by an audience on separate slips of paper. They put these slips into a hat. Examples are things like "chopping wood," "feeding a baby," "rolling a bowling ball," and "grilling burgers." Each person in the group must write down at least two activities and put them in the hat.

- Next, the facilitator asks two people to stand in front of the full group and draw a suggestion from the hat. Pairs will challenge each other in one-to-one battles of the imagination based on suggestions drawn from the hat.

Person A draws a slip of paper from the hat, reads it out loud to the group, and then mimes the action (e.g., rolling a bowling ball). Person A then challenges the other person in the pair, Person B, to mime the same gesture and 'top' it with a different (and perhaps weirder/wilder) description of what they are doing *with the same gesture.* In other words, Person B will still be miming rolling a bowling ball but would be describing a completely different activity.

A round might go like this:

- Person A (a suggestion by the group, a gesture): "I am rolling a bowling ball."
- Person B (same gesture): "I am playing marbles""
- Person A (same gesture): "I am giving you a low five."
- Person B (same gesture): "I am tossing away my trash."
- Person A (same gesture): "I am returning a turtle to its pond."

- A round ends when one person in the pair fails to come up with a new meaning for the gesture within five seconds.

- The game continues until everyone in the group has been both Person A (who takes the suggestion) and Person B in a pairing or until the allotted time runs out, whichever comes first.

The debrief is a discussion about how the same gesture can be interpreted in multiple ways. If appropriate, the discussion can include examining cultural differences and how the same gestures or body language can be interpreted in different ways by different cultures.

We can stretch our minds to accommodate new contexts for familiar scenarios. We can be creative, even when we are given the constraints of a single gesture. Our imaginations are not bound by our current vocabularies and understandings.

OBJECTIVE: Innovation

DURATION: 1 hour

PHYSICAL ENVIRONMENTS

FRAME: Customer Communication

Our friend Cam Danielson frequently begins a conversation with new clients by posing this question:

What is most important to your business?

Most groups will come up with half a dozen ideas—
Employees
Reputation
Brand
Product
Credit
Strategy
Leadership
—before they get to what Danielson believes is most important to every business:
Customers

Who will buy what you're selling? The answer determines the fate of every enterprise. The game for this frame will help you get good answers by seeing the world through your customers' eyes.

GAME: Be the Customer

Spend the entire day being your customers. Do everything like them and, along the way, keep notes on how you behave, and how it feels, and what you notice. Many of our most productive breakthroughs come when we walk in our customers' shoes. This game is a way to systematically collect insights gained on a one-day walk.

Here's how you play it:

- Each participant will be invited to a shared spreadsheet, such as Google or Excel.

  The shared spreadsheet will have a list of 'known archetypes' for your customers, however you refer to them in your company. Let's say you have four archetypes and that you commonly identify them by these names:

  Normcore
  Artisan
  Seeker
  Influencer

  For each customer archetype, there are three columns in the spreadsheet:

  Behavior
  Feeling
  Insight

In this example, your grid will look like this:

	Behavior	Feeling	Insight
Normcore			
Artisan			
Seeker			
Influencer			

- To begin the game, participants choose one of the archetypes and assume that character's identity for the day. To create an identity, a person doesn't have to get all theatrical about it. They can simply choose to *see and respond to the normal course of the day's events as they imagine their customer's character would.*

  For example, in a water cooler conversation–

  Normcore might respond by extolling the virtues of drinking water.
  Artisan would point out the source of the water.
  Seeker would suggest alternate sources of water.
  Influencer would convince you to flavor your water with lemon juice.

  And so it would go, throughout the day. Participants should update the shared spreadsheet as frequently as possible to create a sense of participation in a living story.

- Every time a participant responds as they believe their customer would, they add an entry to the spreadsheet, one note in each of the three columns. For example, for the water cooler responses, people might note:

Normcore

> Behavior: Enjoyed a drink of water
> Feeling: Satisfaction
> Insight: I like the little things.

Artisan

> Behavior: Expertise on water
> Feeling: Knowledgeable
> Insight: I go deep into a subject.

Seeker

> Behavior: Look for water alternatives
> Feeling: Curiosity
> Insight: I'm never satisfied.

Influencer

> Behavior: Persuaded someone to add lemon juice to water
> Feeling: Accomplishment
> Insight: I can convince people.

- The game is played in the course of an entire day. Everyone in the group of participants is required to make at least three entries for their character type, and to add their entries to the spreadsheet by the end of the day.

On the following day, the facilitator(s) compile the insights from the spreadsheet and share these with the group, and, to the degree that it's helpful, the larger enterprise.

OBJECTIVE: Customer Success

DURATION: 1 day

PHYSICAL AND ONLINE ENVIRONMENTS

FRAME: Customer Curiosity

Are you having problems making meaningful relationships with your customers? This game will help you do that in a whole new way, by being curious and asking questions you haven't asked before using metaphors. Metaphors are powerful because they help us consider new ideas or concepts in a relatable way. They help us move away from talking about features and benefits and towards a better understanding of a customer's core values. You will be using images to get to know your customer better.

GAME: Visual Metaphors

You and your team will be creating a bunch of visual metaphors to illustrate what your customer's core values are. What do they care about? What moves them? Who moves them? Why?

- First, put three or more representations of your brand on large Post-It sheets you've mounted on a wall. You can choose from the following types of representations:

  - Product (an image or name of something you sell)
  - Persona (an image and/or name you've given a type of customer)
  - A Motto or Slogan (language you use to describe your offering to customers)

- Before the session, you will have collected magazines, found objects, wrapping paper, or if you're feeling a bit on the wild and crazy side, the contents of your admin's desk drawer. Do it with kindness and leave a thank you note! Then grab scissors, paper, and glue enough for your participants.

- Divide the full group into teams (can be pairs, individuals, or small groups, depending on the size of your session) and have each team choose one of the representations you've got on the wall.

- Using the material you've provided, each team cuts and glues images and phrases to their representation's Post-It sheet. All these images and phrases are metaphors.

- After teams have created a collage of metaphors around its representation of your brand (15-20 minutes), the full group re-assembles, and teams interpret their metaphors with help from the full group. Each interpretation should answer a meaningful question about your customers, for example:

  - How does a customer find us?
  - How does our product fit into a customer's life?
  - What does our customer hate?
  - What does our customer love?

Once you have landed on an idea, start looking for a visual representation.

For example, if your customer works for a big hotel chain and cares about making you feel welcome, you could start to think about all the things they could do at the hotel to make you want to leave. After you brainstorm a few different ideas, maybe you land on scratchy towels, blankets, and pillows. The group then looks at the material you have at your disposal, and you find a piece of sandpaper. You could use the sandpaper and then draw a big X over it and say, "don't let us rub you the wrong way!"

By using a visual metaphor, you give people a better understanding of the overall concept or meaning. People tend to pay more attention to visuals.

OBJECTIVE: Customer Success

SUGGESTED DURATION: 2 hours

PHYSICAL ENVIRONMENTS

FRAME: Customer Success

There's no bigger challenge to a team than a presentation to a client or stakeholder who can significantly impact the future of your organization. Often, the preparation for these interactions is more focused on outcomes than on process. In other words, your team will devote its prep time to ensure a specific outcome from the interaction instead of focusing on the interaction itself. It's as if you're spending all your time designing a hammer, without regard to what you'll be using it for – driving nails, sculpting, horseshoe-making, or playing whack-a-mole. Don't do that. Do this. Design your hammer to suit its purpose.

GAME: Hammer Time

It's important to prepare for upcoming interactions with clients and stakeholders. We often come to these interactions blindly and they end up biting us in the you-know-what or the you-know-where. Sometimes both.

One way to prepare is to think about all the questions you may get asked and prepare what you would say or how you would respond.

- Start out by writing the six most common beginnings to vital questions: Who, What, When, Where, Why, and How.

- Then have the group think of all the possible Who questions, What questions, Where questions, When questions, Why questions and How questions. Write all these questions down on Post-Its.

- After you feel as if you have exhausted all the possible questions the client or stakeholder might ask, have the group come up with answers for all the questions.

- Finally, 'hammer' the presentation you plan to give in light of the questions you've asked and answered in this game. Adjust your presentation or add notes to it so that you'll be prepared to answer as many of the questions as possible.

This preparation will help you feel more confident when you have your next important interaction with a client or stakeholder. That confidence will, itself, answer the question your audience most wants answered: Do these people know what they're doing?

OBJECTIVE: Communication, Customer Success

SUGGESTED DURATION: 30 mins - 1 hour

PHYSICAL AND ONLINE ENVIRONMENTS

CAN BE PLAYED ASYNCHRONOUSLY

FRAME: Customer Support

Here is an often-heard exchange:

Employee Who Didn't Attend: "How was it?"

Employee Who Attended: (shrugs dismissively) "It turned into a bitch-fest."

Who is bitchier than a bitchy customer? Customer Support teams are rife with legendary stories of customer complaints: the woman who complained about a rash after taking a bath using laundry detergent; the man whose dog lost a claw while he was walking it on your company's treadmill; the raccoon that ate the padding off a car's steering wheel and dashboard because its owner left it unlocked.

We have a simple, 100% guaranteed way to prevent a gathering from turning into a bitchfest.

Call it a Bitchfest to begin with. If it *already is* that, it cannot turn into that. Set out to make your bitching festive and productive, instead of a closet full of specters waiting for their time to invade the room. Here's a game for doing that.

GAME: Complaint Symphony

Sometimes our days are filled with the pleasant sounds of birds singing, children cooing their first words, and customers being delighted, but many other times all we hear is Brraaaackk! Cawwwww! Blechh! Whaa, Whaa, Whaa! *It sucks! You suck! Your company/product/service sucks!*

Problems arise when we aren't listening to understand. Empathetic listening is the only way to fix this scenario and turn the cacophony of complaining customers back into music to our ears.

Here is a great way to get in the minds and better hear the voices of your customers.

- Gather your team and give names (personas) to your chronically complaining customers. Like Rick the Dick, who always has something insulting to say about your product because he's carrying a lot of psychological trauma in his life. Or Sierra the Barbarian who can't seem to use your sophisticated product because she is a brute. Write down all these personas on index cards or sticky notes. One for each card. These personas will come to life and be the 'instruments' in your orchestra of complaining customers.

- Ask four people on the team to come up to the front of the room. Each of them will be assigned a different persona. If there is any hesitation, remind them that no musical talent is necessary; they can be tone-deaf and still slay it! One person will be Sierra; one will be Rick, etc.–you get the idea. These 'customers' will line up, forming a straight line across, facing their audience.

- Next, ask another team member to be the complaint conductor. Each person in the symphony will be making raucous 'music' by taking on that persona and complaining as if they were him, her, or them. Get into their shoes and feel what it feels like to be them. The conductor will be pointing to different people at different times and cueing you to get louder, softer, more enraged, etc. Together, these voices compose a customer complaint symphony.

- Notes:

    - Don't speak unless you are pointed at.
    - You must speak the entire time you are pointed at.
    - The conductor will make you speak louder and softer by raising or lowering a pointed hand.
    - When the conductor wants you to stop, they will make a sweeping gesture at you with their hand. Keep talking until the conductor silences you.
    - The conductor may cue any number of people to be talking at the same time.
    - Keep time. Each symphony should last between two and three minutes.

- After each 'performance,' discuss ideas that came out of being the voice of a complaining customer or hearing the customer in a different way. Is there something you hadn't thought of that could lead to a better solution? Improve your process?

- Give these notes on your (proposed) improvements to each of the people playing a complaining customer and ask them to consider them in light of their complaints.

- Conduct the symphony again with the same people as complainers/conductor. Note and discuss any differences in the voices of the complaining customers. Are the new voices more musical? More pleasing to the ear? Less strident?

- Codify the proposed improvements that sound to the group as if they've made the biggest, most positive differences to the symphony.

- Continue playing the game until everyone in the group has had a chance to play two different personas, or one persona and the conductor. Or until you run out of time, whichever comes first.

An organization is like an orchestra. The vibrations caused by interactions with your customers are a form of music. It's up to you to do the tuning, eliminate the sour notes, and create the harmonies to attract and hold your audience.

OBJECTIVE: Communication, Customer Success

SUGGESTED DURATION: 2 hours

PHYSICAL AND ONLINE ENVIRONMENTS

FRAME: Decision Making

You've brainstormed brilliantly. You've expanded the possibilities for you and your team. The diversity of thinking, the number of voices heard, the flights of serendipity and the sweet serenity of a creative session conducted without judgment are all on full display on hundreds of sticky notes stuck to the wall, in a bunch of different categories, ranked according to all sorts of criteria, along multiple time frames. The artist in the corner has even drawn a beautiful collage that captures the fervent spirit of this time together.

Now what?

It was great and all, but will we still love one another tomorrow? Who decides what's next? The same people do, that's who. Now that you've diverged in all directions, it's time to converge and decide on a direction that holds the most promise for the road ahead. Here's a game for that.

GAME: Pursue, Pivot, Punt

You have a gazillion ideas, so now what? You could close your eyes and randomly pick something, but that may lead you in a sketchy direction. Instead of going in blind, try this game. This gets the team to narrow down ideas after you have brainstormed.

- Give each part participant red, green, and yellow adhesive dots, ten of each color.

- First, write all your ideas on index cards or sticky notes so that they can be separated, shuffled, moved around. One idea per card. The group will work on getting all the ideas into the following three categories: **Pursue, Pivot, Punt.**

- Each person will get to assign a color dot to each card: **Pursue (green), Pivot (yellow), Punt (red).** You will all get your red, yellow, and green dots, and assign a dot to each one. Once everyone has assigned a dot to each idea card, have someone in the group count the number of dots on each card and place them in the correct category that corresponds with the color dots it has the most of.

- You can have this as a slide or on a flip chart in the room for people to use as reference:

  - **Pursue (green):** An idea we are ready and willing to implement
  - **Pivot (yellow):** A direction worth exploring, but we're not ready to implement
  - **Punt (red):** Discards

- Once everyone in the group has assigned a dot to every idea, group the ideas according to their most-voted category. Spend 10-15 minutes discussing why ideas were voted into each category. What patterns can you see? What are the key differences in the ideas listed for each category?

- Put the **Punt** items into a backlog.

- For each item in the **Pivot** category, co-write a short description of what the pivot might be. For example, if the group feels that sustainability practices at your company are a needed pivot, but don't know what, exactly, the pivot can be, list possible pivots: paper straws and bamboo utensils instead of plastic; a ride-sharing program; more electric chargers in parking lots, etc.

- Finally, roadmap each of the **Pursue** items with key benchmarks such as budgets, schedules, and business objectives. (This can, optionally, be done post-game.)

With the group's discussion and consensus on ideas and roadmapped next steps, you can move forward pronto. Giddyup!

OBJECTIVE: Communication, Strategy

SUGGESTED DURATION: 3 hours

PHYSICAL AND ONLINE ENVIRONMENTS

FRAME: Design Thinking

Design Thinking, which originated with Stanford University's Design School (or 'D-School' as the locals call it), has swept through the surrounding tech valleys and vales like a kind of creative contagion. A happy flu. Everybody designs everything all the time. Your little pony and my little pony, all the little ponies, hoping to grow up to be unicorns one day.

At its most fundamental, the way Design Thinking works is this—we get all our cleverest people in a room, and a facilitator from a place like Stanford or Ideo or The Unicorn Riding Academy guides us in defining some future event we'd like to see come true. Let's say it's 'Björk is Secretary-General of the U.N.'

Once we've defined the future event, we list all the design problems that have to be solved to make that future a reality. For example, if Björk is ever going to be Secretary-General of the U.N., we might decide that we have to convince more people to dress like swans. You know, like Björk.

Then we go about designing solutions to all the problems that must be resolved for our desired future to gallop into our lives like a team of unicorns pulling a golden carriage. How do we get more people to dress like swans? Maybe we'll assign it to a committee. Yeah, that's it. We'll appoint a Committee to Promote Swan Couture. Okay, that problem is solved. And on we go to the next problem, and the next, and so on, until we have solved every problem that would keep Björk from becoming Secretary-General of the U.N. At which point, Björk, would pretty much get the job. Design Thinking, ladies, and gentlemen. You're welcome.

GAME: Design Thinkeroo

For our game, you're going to play with Design Thinking, but we don't want you or your team to think about a grand or far-off or extravagant future. This game has the near future as its destination and immediate practicality as its focus.

It can be played solo, or in a group. It can be played at any time, day or night, in any location. The playing field is your mind.

- First, imagine a future shift that's near-at-hand, meaning you can affect it, and soon. It will be an incremental improvement on your current status quo, a future world that's a tiny bit better than the world you're living in now. What is it? A better breakfast routine? A less cluttered desk? A little less sass from the kiddos?

- Hold this desired future firmly in your imagination. Set it as a clear and focused intention.

- Now think of how many ways your world might

change for the better with this future that's only slightly different from your present. For example, a better breakfast routine might result in improved health, weight loss, better energy to start the day, a better relationship with your partner, a lighter healthier lunch, getting out of bed earlier, a change in your diet, better planning, etc. Whatever it is, a future that's better by a fraction can have lots of implications. Realize that.

- Now define one problem that can bring about your desired future if you design a solution for it. For example, if your desired future is 'A better breakfast routine,' perhaps the problem to be solved is that you only eat breakfast sporadically. In that case, the solution is to make sure you eat breakfast every day. Voila. Problem solved. Future with a better breakfast routine assured.

- Set the solution to the problem as the practice that will be the bridge between you and your desired future. Cross that bridge as often as it takes until your desired future is realized.

Somewhere, Björk will be munching on a gluten-free bagel, and she'll know. She'll know.

OBJECTIVE: Innovation

DURATION: 30 min - 1 hour

PHYSICAL AND ONLINE ENVIRONMENTS

FRAME: Diversity and Inclusion

Do I know you? Most people rely on their past knowledge and assume they know things about people before they ever get to know them deeply. This way of thinking often causes barriers or misconceptions about what the people on your team are really like and what they can bring to the table. In the game below, the group will start to bust open assumptions and find out who the people around them really are.

GAME: I'm Someone Who

At least two days before the gathering, give everyone a copy of the *"I'm someone who..."* handout (below).

- People are to come to the game having filled in the blanks in the handout on their own time.

- Participants pair up with people from their team or different departments and are asked to share their responses. Ask them to note differences between their previous perceptions of one another and what their responses are.

- When all the pairs have filled in all the blanks, have the full group discuss what they noticed about the exercise. What are the differences between perceptions and realities? How might this affect how we interact with one another?

The word 'prejudice' is rooted in the Latin words for pre-judging. Instead of filling in the blanks in a person's story without knowing anything about them, it's much better to assume nothing and get to know them first. Listen first. We often lead with assumptions when it's much more generous and collaborative and ultimately productive to lead with curiosity.

OBJECTIVE: Communication, Collaboration

SUGGESTED DURATION: 1 hour

PHYSICAL AND ONLINE ENVIRONMENTS

I Am Someone Who

I am someone who loves _____.

I am someone who dislikes _____.

I am someone who can _____.

I am someone who cannot _____.

I am someone who always_____.

I am someone who never _____.

I am someone who tries to _____.

I am someone who wishes _____.

FRAME: Emotional Connection

As we become more geographically dispersed as organizations and teams ... as we gather more and more data about one another so that our stats become our identities ... as intelligent machines take over more and more of the operational aspects of work ... as we mask our faces and safe our spaces ... it has never been more important that we relate to one another as human beings.

Our human connections are primarily emotional. As Maya Angelou said, "I've learned that people will forget what you said, people will forget what you did, but people will never forget how you made them feel."

GAME: Masks and Expressions

This game will remind us that there's an emotion lurking behind every facial expression. Even when that expression includes a mask, we can discern clues to a person's inner life. Sensing and respecting these clues is an essential aspect of human communication. Here's a game designed specifically for the online space:

- Everyone will need to bring their *COVID mask* to the call. The game begins with *no one wearing a mask.*

- Players can either be assigned a number, take turns, or given another way to know when it's their turn to be 'it.'

- One at a time, each person in the group gets a turn putting on their mask. They are to make one of four facial expressions behind their mask: Smile / Frown / Neutral / Wild Card. A Wild Card can be any expression that's not one of the other three. (At the facilitator's option, players can be given a couple of minutes to prep Wild Card expressions by looking at a page of animation facial expressions, which are easily findable on the web.)

- In the chat window, others in the group enter their guesses of the expression the person wears behind their mask. Players who guess 'Wild Card' must also name the emotion conveyed by the expression. (At the facilitator's option, these guesses can either be visible to the entire group, or visible only to a scorekeeper.)

- Players receive one point for correctly guessing the expression behind the mask, and five bonus points if they correctly name the emotion conveyed by a Wild Card expression.

- The game continues like this until all the players have taken a turn. The scorekeeper totals the scores; a winner is named. The rest of the group honors the winner by making a Totally Inappropriate Expression in their honor.

Play this game a couple of times, and you'll never look at a masked person the same way again or take a person's emotions for granted.

OBJECTIVE: Communication

DURATION: 30 mins

ONLINE ENVIRONMENTS

FRAME: Escalation

Any worthwhile story has what we call 'dynamic range.' This means that a story, like life itself, does not unfold along a straight line or smooth curve. There are ups and downs. Twists and turns. This is true, too, for business stories. As much as we'd like every day to be mathematically predictable, no day is. There are as many changes in tone, tempo, and emotional pitch in a typical day as there are in an Octavia Butler novel.

One of the most familiar dynamics is escalation–what improvisers call 'heightening.' This happens when the emotional pitch of a scene rises, tempo increases, and the stakes grow higher. Escalation is a familiar dynamic for Customer Service operations when a problem cannot be resolved in an initial conversation with a call center or by the first line of customer responses. Escalation happens formally or informally in all businesses. It is a critical dynamic when everyday issues can blow up into crises with costly outcomes.

How does one prepare for escalation? Like one prepares for anything–with practice! This is a way to prepare for the scenarios that can cost you needless time and money, demoralize your people, and deflate your brand's reputation in the eyes of your customers.

In other words, you're going to prepare for the worst to be your best.

GAME: To Make Matters Worse

Note that there are positive as well as negative escalations. Not every escalation has the potential to become a crisis. Closing a big deal or winning a bid come with their own kind of escalation. Because we're dealing with possible crisis scenarios here, this game is primarily for negative escalations. Feel free to adapt it for different kinds of escalations.

- A group of up to 20 people comes up with *ten business scenarios* that can result in escalation.

- The group breaks into pairs, and each pair picks one of the scenarios. One person plays the Customer, and one plays the Company.

  The Customer begins by stating the escalation scenario and adding to it with a new statement that starts with "To make matters worse…"

  The player speaking for the Company responds. It's no use. The response does not make things better. The Customer comes back with another statement that makes matters even worse.

  Again the Company responds. And for a third time, the Customer responds in a way that makes things worse, still, to the point where the scenario has become a crisis.

- The players then spend a few minutes discussing and listing at least one more move that would have de-escalated the scenario and averted or diminished the crisis.

- The players then switch Customer and Company roles and repeat the "To make matters worse…" cycle with a new scenario from the list of ten. This continues for 20 more minutes.

- Participants spend the second half of the game, approximately 30 minutes, sharing their scenarios and their solutions for de-escalation.

Good teams compete in any type of arena, from the soccer pitch to the marketplace, they practice and prepare for as many scenarios as possible, especially those most likely to impede their performance. Get ready. Then go!

OBJECTIVE: Communication, Strategy

DURATION: 1 hour

PHYSICAL AND ONLINE ENVIRONMENTS

CAN BE PLAYED ASYNCHRONOUSLY

FRAME: Expressing Creativity

Our friend, music producer Jo Curbishly, uses the phrase 'cleansing creativity' to describe a company she started to combine body scrubbing and yoga. We think 'cleansing' is a brilliant metaphor for becoming more creative. Cleanse whatever gets in the way of your creativity. Instead of focusing on your creativity, focus on eliminating 'anti-creative' behaviors from your approach to a problem. Creativity wants to happen, and if nature is allowed to take its course, it will happen, because nature itself is creative. Just don't get in her way, and she'll take care of the rest.

Another friend of ours, Denise Jacobs, writes about this process in her book, *Banish Your Inner Critic*. Sometimes our thoughts about our process are the single biggest impediment to the process itself.

This frame is where you release creativity with a game designed to remove the things that get in its way: Yes-butting, Judgment, Doubt, Completion Anxiety, Poor Process Design, etc.

GAME: Inner Critic Coffee

Most of us human folk deal with this little fellow inside of our heads who loves to tell us just how wrong we are. Most of us have this critical part of ourselves who comes out when we are stressed, saying things like, "Idiot. You're so dumb, why did you do that?" and "It's wonderful– not!" In this game, we are going to confront these demons over coffee. Instead of pretending none of us have these little nagging voices in our heads, we are going to wear them on the outside. We are literally going to become them.

- Before coming into this caffeinated arena, ask each participant to come up with a name for their inner critic.

- When they arrive, each person will be given a name tag and a Sharpie and asked to write their inner critic's name on their name tag.

- Conduct your coffee conclave with a normal business agenda. Keep your regular order of business. The only adjustment is that each person will be speaking and responding as their inner critic.

  For example, if your inner critic is Red Pen Rhoda, who edits what you say or before you say or write it, you will embody her. And you are going to criticize everyone's choice of language, including your own. You might want to point at them with a red Sharpie when you do.

  If your inner critic is "Procrastinating Parvesh," you're going to be the person who advocates for not doing anything or doing it in an overly cautious or deliberate way. You get the idea. You will still have the same business agenda as you normally would, but the people attending are a lot more CRITICAL of everyone and everything. And DRAMATIC with their dialogue!

- Spend ten minutes at the end of Inner Critic Coffee discussing how these negative thoughts can: 1) derail our thinking; and 2) adversely affect a group. How do the voices inside our heads influence our spoken or written communication? How does negative thinking kill creativity before it has had a chance to blossom? How are creativity and criticism paired in productive scenarios, and how is it different from how they're paired in unproductive scenarios?

This gathering is about calling out our inner critics by over-dramatizing them. The next time the negative little nabobs inside our heads try to tell us we aren't good enough, it will be easier to laugh them off and re-write them out of existence by replacing them with the voices of characters who are more encouraging, supportive, and open to our ideas.

OBJECTIVE: Innovation, Communication

DURATION: 1 hour

PHYSICAL AND ONLINE ENVIRONMENTS

FRAME: Expressing Gratitude

Probably the single biggest gripe we hear from employees is that their work goes unrecognized and that people are not appreciated for the value they bring to an organization, especially in ways that don't show up on a spreadsheet. These ways are vital to a group's culture and performance. The most common reason we hear from employees looking to change companies is, "I want to be somewhere where I'm appreciated."

Managers who have the attitude of "We show our thanks by giving you a paycheck," are soon managing teams composed of hangers-on with low self-esteem, people who are only in it for the paycheck and will only do the minimum required to collect it, and rookies hired to replace people who leave because they're in it for more than the paycheck. In other words, the best employees leave because they feel unrecognized and underappreciated.

GAME: Thank You For

"Thank you" is nice to hear but saying thank you for something specific is even better. This is a simple day-long game that will open your eyes and ears to opportunities for expressing gratitude.

- Focus on honoring the small contributions people make every day that you might typically overlook.

Take note and respond. What do you notice? What impact does it have? Why are you grateful for it?

- Every thank-you counts. No move is too small to merit gratitude. Make sure to address people directly. You will make their day happier.

- Make today a day of giving thanks and see if you can work up to making more and more days filled with gratitude.

Thank-yous are multipliers. Eventually, this simple game can inspire many different appreciative experiences and expressions of gratitude in your company. There is no reason why this game cannot be played every day.

OBJECTIVE: Collaboration, Communication

DURATION: 1 day

PHYSICAL AND ONLINE ENVIRONMENTS

FRAME: Final Review

There's a lot of sloppy editing going on out there. A lot of content that gets shipped without attention to detail. In our opinion, this sloppiness is tied to the tempo at which business gets conducted. A network's appetite for information is constant and insatiable. In the never-ending rush to ship work, quality control is an issue. Writers are asked to edit their own work. Developers review their own code. Manufacturers examine the quality control of their products. This is never as effective as viewing the content with a fresh set of eyes.

Artificial Intelligence can't catch every mistake. Filter the following sentence through spell and grammar check. It sails through untouched: *Short sentences that look like biased AI, and you get sentencing that looks like this.* The appearance of meaning is more important to a learning machine than meaning itself.

This game is your hedge against dumb mistakes. Every parent has blind spots concerning their child, and every creator is the same way with their creation. Get a fresh-eyed group together to review your work before it goes out into the world. Play this game.

GAME: Fresh Eyes

When a CEO flaps her wings, cars make U-turns on busy streets in distant cities, and dogs get sent to kennels because their owners have to catch planes. Companies launching a new product or producing a big event want to limit the CEO wing-flapping. A pre-flap game is in order.

Imagine that your group is responsible for a shareholders' meeting tomorrow. You're planning everything from who's on the guest list, to where they'll sit, to what they'll be eating, to the content they'll be sharing. There are lots of moving pieces in scenarios like this and lots of domino effects when there are slip-ups in your performance. In situations like these, preparation is just as important as planning. This game will better prepare you and your team to deliver on your vision.

Sometimes we are so bogged down in our own work that we can't see things that are obvious to a fresh pair of eyes.

- Have everyone come together with what they have been working on and get into a circle around the table.

- Then each person will pass their portion of work to the person sitting on his or her right. That person will look over the work for a few minutes and present it aloud to the full group. They will note any questions or feedback that they have for the original content creator.

- Pass your content two more times. Each time, the work gets presented aloud by a new presenter, and each time it must 'run the gauntlet' of compliments, commentary, critique, and suggestions by the full group.

This game will get you prepped and ready to run the gauntlet. Your CEO will be flapping her wings in the direction you want for your organization! Flap, my pretties, FLAAAAAPPPPPPP!

OBJECTIVE: Innovation, Collaboration, Communication

SUGGESTED DURATION: 1 hour

PHYSICAL AND ONLINE ENVIRONMENTS

CAN BE PLAYED ASYNCHRONOUSLY

FRAME: Forecasting

We use a lot of improvisation techniques in our work. These techniques bring the skills used by musical, theatrical, and comedic improvisers into other arenas, a practice known as Applied Improvisation. With these techniques, people learn how to connect in ways that will result in better collaborations, and, ultimately, in individual and group transformation. The group affects the individual; the individual affects the group; individuals affect one another. Possibilities abound.

One aspect of improvisation that is especially applicable in other contexts is the way that improvisers make bets on the future. They understand how their actions in the present are likely to affect the future, and how to make smart bets that are likely to pay off.

In this practice, preparation is more important than predictions. Improvisers understand that, even when they're on the same page on stage, unexpected events can change the course of a scene or a show. This can happen when a scene is falling flat and needs energy, bigger stakes, heightened emotions. It can happen when an unexpected opportunity presents itself, and it's too good to pass up. The entire performance can be made memorable for an audience with just one such move. The point, in either case, is to be ready. We know how to prepare for the weather. Why not be as prepared for the future of our work?

GAME: What's the Weather Like?

A weather forecast is a statement of expected future occurrences. Weather forecasting includes the use of objective data and the skill and experience of those doing the forecasting. There's a certain amount of intuition involved.

Why do we watch or listen to a weather forecast, or check the weather app on our phone? One reason is to be prepared. Dress appropriately, make travel plans, decide on what kind of odds we'll have of staying dry if we attend an outdoor event, decide what kind of vacation we'll be taking. A weather forecast takes an immense pool of data and simplifies it into recognizable conditions–cold fronts, high pressure zones, chances of rain. This game can do the same with the immense pool of data you have on your company's or community's future. This game will help you simplify that data, put it in terms people can readily understand and prepare for.

Do this with your upcoming project roadmap. Build a weather forecast to help your internal team understand where you are headed in the next few months–what type of 'atmosphere' you can expect for your project and how best to prepare for it. Give fair warning for anticipated changes in conditions. That's what this forecast is all about. Don't let them get caught in the rain or hit in the head with golf-ball-sized hail.

- First, let's build a vocabulary of weather terms, and what they mean when we use them as metaphors for our work:

ALTIMETER - The visibility of your project and group within your organization.

BAROMETRIC PRESSURE - The pressure exerted by forces outside a group's or company's control.

BLIZZARD - Dangerous conditions for going anywhere or doing anything. Do *not* get caught outside in one. Rescue dogs may be required. This is a good time to bake cookies.

CHINOOK - A type of warm wind. Also known as the Snow Eater. Also, a helicopter. Also, a salmon. Who knew??

CLIMATE - The historical record and description of daily and seasonal events that help describe a company's or community's culture. The status quo. The operating environment in which a project will be produced.

CLOUD - A visible collection of matter that obscures our vision.

COLD FRONT - The leading edge of an advancing cold air mass that is displacing the warmer air in its path. A clash. It can be a signal for sweater weather. Get your earmuffs ready.

CURRENT - A flow of events and people going in a particular direction.

DOG DAYS - The naturally occurring slowdown when Europeans and network executives go on vacation, and it's hard to get a decision out of anyone.

DROUGHT - Deadly dry spell. Precipitation needed!

EL NIÑO - Warm flows replace cold and bring with them new dynamics and possibilities

FLOOD - An overflow of events that cannot be contained by current structures, safeguards, or lifeguards. Inundation and submersion ensue.

HAIL - Precipitation in the shape of a frozen ball that can hurt you if it hits you.

HEATWAVE - Things heat up to the point of discomfort for an extended period. Children look for water hoses to play with.

HUMIDITY - The amount of water vapor in the air. It is often confused with relative humidity or dew point. Types of humidity include absolute humidity, relative humidity, and specific humidity. Florida is full of this!! #thefrizzyhairmaker

ICE STORM - A severe condition, hazardous to any movement. Causes utility problems. Things don't work.

JET STREAM - Strong winds that can slow you down, speed you up or turn you sideways, depending on which direction you're heading.

LIGHTNING - A big jolt of energy. Can be frightening.

MONSOON - A seasonal downpour.

NOR'EASTER - Notoriously bad weather ahead.

OVERCAST - The amount of sky cover for a cloud layer.

PRECIPITATION - Fluidity in different forms. Necessary for growth. Too much, or the wrong form at the wrong time, can hurt you.

RAIN - Life-giving substance.

SATURATE - To treat or charge something to the point where no more can be absorbed, dissolved, or retained.

TEMPERATURE - The measure of molecular motion or the degree of heat of a substance.

THUNDERSTORM - Turbulent conditions

TIDE - The periodic or cyclical changes that can be expected in an organization or community. Marked by regularly scheduled events and a dynamic of 'rising' and 'falling.'

TORNADO - A violently rotating event or pivot with an overpowering centrifugal force that could suck your entire office out of Kansas and land it in Munchkinville. Seek shelter underground! Or in a ditch!

TSUNAMI - A long wave of extended change formed by a cataclysmic event that is usually unseen by those who will be affected by the change.

UPDRAFT - A small-scale current of air that produces lift. Contrast with a downdraft.

WARM FRONT - A thaw, a heating-up. Things are moving and changing.

WIND - A flow of events with four indicators: direction, speed, character (severity), and shifts.

- Working as a team, use these terms (you can invite people to add others from any weather wiki) to build three forecasts for your project: 7-day, 30-day, 3-month.

- Once you've built the forecasts, have fun delivering them in the manner of your favorite TV weather personalities. Make maps. Use extravagant hand gestures in your presentations to indicate expected conditions. Let your forecasts answer questions such as what 'season' you're in, what conditions will be challenging, and what will be conducive to growth. Is it time to cover a lot of ground, or time to hunker down and weather a storm?

- After giving the forecasts, make a list of preparations for each of the forecasts. What must your group do to prepare for the predicted conditions? By adding these preparations and contingencies to your roadmap, you'll improve your odds of success by improving your ability to adapt to conditions that are beyond your control, but which will affect your team and its work.

We are all subject to forces in our environment that are beyond our control. In this game, the weather is a metaphor for forces that affect us at work. We adapt to weather conditions. Those adaptations are also a metaphor for how you and your Doppler Radar Team can adapt and work productively in all kinds of conditions.

OBJECTIVE: Communication, Strategy

SUGGESTED DURATION: 3 hours

PHYSICAL AND ONLINE ENVIRONMENTS

FRAME: Gaining Clarity

Often, when we get tangled up in a complicated problem or fail to meet a challenge, it's because we keep looking at it through the same lens, with the same textual and verbal descriptions. We keep wracking our brain for an answer our brain didn't create. This game will give you the benefit of using different visual metaphors to see the problem differently and arrive together at fresh ideas for resolving it.

GAME: Alchemy

Sometimes a situation is so complex, with so many variables, it can feel impossible to know with any certainty how to proceed. This is why an ancient sage first coined the phrase 'Cannot see the forest for the trees.' When everything in our frame of reference is worthy, on its own, of our attention, we can be blinded to the big picture. Based on the alchemical principle of 'distillation,' this exercise was created by Dr. Debra Hockenberry-Salsi, chair of the SEAM doctoral program at the University of Lyon, and an expert in business transformation. We're sharing it with her permission.

The game is best played in two parts, over two days.

- On Day One / Part One, a person in the group who is responsible for 'managing the complexity' is to take ten minutes (and only ten, if you need to assign a timekeeper, do it) to *draw a picture of the problem* on an 8.5"x11" sheet of paper. The person can use any medium–crayons, markers, pens, paints etc.–to draw the picture. The only other rule, aside from the paper's size and the time limit, is that no words are allowed in the drawing. Only images. Be vulnerable. Don't think about it. Just draw it.

- When the ten minutes are up, the person immediately *scans the drawing and shares it* with the rest of the group.

- In preparation for Day Two / Part Two, each person in the group is asked to *'lighten' the drawing* they've been sent. In essence, this means adding life and clarity to the original drawing that helps make sense of it. This act of illumination can mean whatever a person wants it to mean–seeing a pattern or patterns; simplifying it by giving it an overall shape or composition; tearing it to pieces and putting it back together again in a different way. There's no limit to how the 'lightening' can strike. Again, no words should be used in this phase of the game.

- The group convenes on Day Two / Part Two. The person who did the original drawing begins by sharing it on camera with the group and explaining it to whatever degree they feel is necessary with feelings, themes, ideas, and structures that went into it–like a chef describing a recipe.

- Each person in the group takes turns sharing their 'lightened' drawings and explaining their own process–like a second chef who took the original recipe and made it their own. For each of these drawings, the group discusses how they might help simplify, clarify and/or resolve the depicted problem. What looks easier? What is revealed? What patterns repeat? What fades into the background or moves to the foreground? Questions and observations can be converted into a plan of action.

OBJECTIVE: Communication, Customer Success, Strategy

SUGGESTED DURATION: 90 mins (over two days)

PHYSICAL AND ONLINE ENVIRONMENTS

CAN BE PLAYED ASYNCHRONOUSLY

FRAME: Getting Unstuck

Who hasn't found themselves stuck on an idea, a story, or the approach to solving a problem, and never seem to get anywhere? We keep banging our heads against the wall with ideas that don't connect, tried-and-true formulas that don't work, and resistance from above. What if we could change things by letting our responses to our environment tell us what to do next? We are in luck. Here's a way to get unstuck.

GAME: Chilean Miner Escape Act

On August 6, 2010, 33 men working in a gold mine outside Copiapo, Chile, were trapped in a mine collapse. Sixty-nine days later, in an event seen broadcast live around the world, they were rescued. What happened in the intervening days made the miracle rescue possible.

This game is based on three things the miners did to set the stage for their rescue: took on clearly defined roles, used available resources, and got help from above.

- *Step One: Define Your Predicament*

  The first move in the Chilean Miner Escape Act is to define the nature of your 'entrapment.' Where are you stuck? The Chilean Miners knew everything about that mine. They knew how far underground they were. They knew how much air they'd have to breathe. How many days their food and water would last. What different sounds inside the mine indicated. Among the 33 of them, they had complementary skills for enduring their ordeal. They were also realists. They knew what would have to happen for them to make it out alive.

For 30 minutes, your group is going to mirror them, and define everything you can about your own predicament, with emphasis on hard facts. Put these facts on Post-it notes on a wall, in three categories: Available Resources, Danger Signals, and What's Needed.

- *Step Two: Assume Your Roles*

To get unstuck, all 33 of the miners took on roles that complemented one another, and honored each man's unique skills. Note that these roles were different from the roles they played in their normal work lives. These roles were *specifically suited to the problem* of surviving long enough to give them a chance of making it out of the mine alive. Daniel Herrera was a truck driver who became a medic for the men and monitored their mental states. Florencia Avalos went from being a miner to a videographer. Edison Peña ran 10K a day underground and led the men in maintaining their physical stamina. And so it was for all 33 of them, each with a role that would be supportive of the group.

For the next 30 minutes, your group will mirror the miners, and define roles for yourselves that are related to solving your predicament. Each role must be different, and each role should complement at least one other role. There is no ranking or status associated with the roles. They are in relation to the process of getting unstuck from the predicament you're in. Roles will take on different status depending on which aspects of the problem are being addressed at the time. We are all subject matter experts in something. These roles should be defined to bring as much subject matter expertise as possible to bear on the situation at hand.

Make a column of your roles in Post-it notes on the wall that will look like this:

- When the group has arrived at a list of roles that are all unique, complementary, and related to the process for solving the problem, make a second identical column, so that the wall will look like this, with the same eight roles listed in both columns, in the same order:

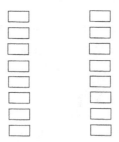

- Next, draw lines between roles that are complementary with one another. For example, if one Role #1 is 'Guinea Pig,' complementary roles might be Role #3 ('Lab Manager') and Role #6 ('Scientist').' If Role #2 is "Firestarter,' a complementary Role might be Role #4 ('Firefighter') etc.

  Your wall will look something like this:

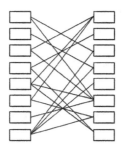

- *Step Three: Get Outside Help*

  The 33 miners knew they weren't going to get out of that mine on their own. They did not have the capability by themselves to dig their way out of there. They'd need outside help, and they got it, in the form of drillers, government officials, media, medical professionals, families, and clerics. The Oakley sportswear company even managed to get 33 pairs of specially-designed sunglasses down to the miners before their rescue so that their eyes could adjust to the sudden glare of work lights, sunlight, and camera lights.

For the next 30 minutes of your game, make a list of the 'outside help' you'll need to get you out of your predicament. Make another list to go on the wall– of the help you're requesting from both inside and outside your organization.

- *Step Four: Have Faith*

  One of the biggest reasons the miners were able to survive and emerge from the mine in relatively healthy condition after being trapped for 69 days of claustrophobic darkness, is that they had faith. In their God. In their families and friends. In their company and their country. They counted on their faith to see them through, even when there was no logical reason to believe they'd get rescued.

  For the next segment of the game, each person in the group will spend five minutes reflecting on 'life outside the problem,' and what it is about that life that sustains them.

  The group then shares its 'items of faith.' This is the culmination of the game. The emotional high point. The consecration of the actions to be taken after more than two months in total darkness.

The group now has everything it needs to approach the predicament in a brand-new way. People can begin adapting their process using the inventory from the Chilean Miner game to help them adjust to their environment, and escape whatever has them trapped for the time being.

OBJECTIVE: Communication, Strategy

DURATION: Full Day

PHYSICAL AND ONLINE ENVIRONMENTS

FRAME: Goal Setting

Alan Kay, computer scientist, Apple Fellow, and inspiration for the character of Alan Bradley in the motion picture, *Tron*, has said, "The best way to predict the future is to create it." So how do we go about creating the future? First, we must envision it. What do you see? Is your future so bright that you have to wear shades to make out its details? Is it gloomy and lacking illumination? It's hard to create a future if you don't have a plan for getting there. Everyone needs to be thinking about the future and what they would like to achieve personally and as a team. Part of thinking about your future is thinking about what challenges you're willing to take on, and what problems you'll need to resolve to achieve your goals. We often need to put clear systems in place to reach those future goals. Those systems will help you have a clear image in your crystal ball.

GAME: Crystal Balls

- Dim the lights before everyone gathers in the room.

- Participants are given the handout below—of a crystal ball they will use to define good fortune in the future. Prior to the game, you will have curated a list of 3-5 questions. They will be composed of:

    - Questions frequently asked by the people who are in the room.

- Questions frequently asked in your organization or community.
- Questions frequently asked in your industry or region.

• Read one question at a time to the group and ask them to write their responses inside their crystal ball. They are to focus their responses on predictions of good fortune about the future. Encourage people to make predictions that are fantastic, extravagant, imaginative, wildly lucrative for themselves and their company, supportive of their community, and good to the planet.

Use examples of extravagant, good fortunes, such as these:

Q: What investments will our company be making in my personal growth in the next two years?

GOOD FORTUNE: They will pay for me to take Ron Howard's online course in film direction and will include a field trip to Hollywood to meet Ron Howard.

Or–

Q: How can we improve our recruitment process to attract talent from other parts of the country?

GOOD FORTUNE: Advertise at music festivals from a branded solar-powered airship that I will pilot.

• When everyone has finished writing down their answers to a question, they take turns reading from their crystal balls.

- After sharing their good fortune (answer) they describe work they're currently doing that can either *help make the good fortune come true* or *keep the good fortune from happening.* These descriptions get written down *outside* the crystal ball on the person's sheet of paper.

- The full group then comments on how the *system* they're in can either help make the good fortune come true or keep it from happening. The person who made the prediction writes down the group's comments outside the crystal ball on their printout.

- This repeats until everyone in the room has shared their predicted good fortune, and how their work can bring it about or hinder it and added the full group's 'system' comments.

- Next, without repeating the good fortunes, the group *recaps all the comments.* They note which comments relate to more than one person's good fortune.

- Finally, they vote on their favorite comment. This is an *agreed-to change to the current system or work process.*

- This cycle of play is repeated for between three and five questions posed to the full group. The objective is to arrive at one agreed-to system/process change for each question posed.

Will these changes produce the fantastic good fortunes predicted by the people playing the game? Will an aviation enthusiast wind up piloting his company's airship when they currently don't have a clue how to pilot an airship, and their company doesn't have an airship? Not likely. Will the changes produce positive outcomes in the future that could not have been envisioned before people look into their crystal balls? Indubitably!

Try not to blink or to look away. Hold your gaze. Good fortune is right around the corner.

OBJECTIVE: Communication, Collaboration

SUGGESTED DURATION: 1 hour

PHYSICAL AND ONLINE ENVIRONMENTS

CAN BE PLAYED ASYNCHRONOUSLY

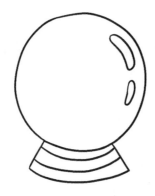

FRAME: Group Alignment

Lately, everyone has been sailing their own vessel; it's a regular regatta around your place, characterized by competition and cross-purposes. Time to gather everyone together, get them aboard the same ship, point them in the same direction, and give them focus and a sense of purpose.

All aboard, mates!

GAME: Oceans Away

- Assemble the team. You'll need a whiteboard (or sheet of easel paper), sticky notes, and black pens.

- Draw an ocean, a sailboat floating on the ocean, and a couple of anchors. If you are the artistic type, feel free to add some flair (we like fish).

- Hand the pens and sticky notes to each of the attendees and ask them to write down the bad things (or issues) and good things (or efficiencies) that have been discovered since the last retrospective. Give everyone five to ten minutes to write down their ideas, thoughts, and/or opinions – encourage the team to participate.

- After everyone is finished, put the sticky notes on the sailboat – the good things represent wind in the sails, and the bad things represent the anchors that slow the boat.

- Once the sticky notes have been placed, have the team organize them into themes or simply groups of like items (e.g., issues surrounding quality).

- Eliminate duplicates and consolidate where possible. Within each theme, rank the different sticky notes.

- Now the team should discuss each top-ranked item and identify issues that need to be worked and/or stories to add to the backlog.

OBJECTIVE: Collaboration, Communication, Strategy

SUGGESTED DURATION: 1-2 hours

PHYSICAL AND ONLINE ENVIRONMENTS

FRAME: Group Empathy

A camera can conceal as much as it reveals. When working remotely we often miss cues that people are getting burnt out, or why, and on top of it, we may have no earthly idea what motivates them and gives them a little pep in their step, what adds the 'go' to their 'get up and–' This is a great way to get to know people on your team on a deeper level. Oh, and you, too. This will help you get to know yourself. We don't want you to get burned out either, and wondering why!

GAME: What Fills Me Up?

We suggest playing this game quickly and debriefing it slowly in small and large group conversations.

- Begin by having each person copy the drawing below. A circle. Two labels. Two arrows.

- Give each person five minutes to list experiences, activities, feelings, or circumstances that deplete them of energy and can lead to burnout. List each of these items *outside the circle*, where your enthusiasm goes to die.

- Then give each person five minutes to list experiences that bring them joy, nurture them, energize them, fill them with enthusiasm. List each of these items *inside the circle*, your radiator of energy and inspiration.

- Ask each person to take a minute to note whether they have more items inside or outside the circle. Ask them to reflect on their responses and on any imbalances and patterns they see in them.

- Next, break out into groups (for an online meeting use the breakout room function) to get the team into pairs or small groups and have them share what fills them up and what depletes them. Give each person at least two minutes to share their responses. Give the breakout groups an additional five minutes to discuss their shared responses. Ask them to identify and discuss themes or patterns their responses have in common.

- Finally, bring the full group back together and take ten minutes to discuss what came up in their breakout rooms, and what it would take for everyone to be so full of enthusiasm, motivation, and commitment that what's inside every person's circle will outweigh whatever's outside it.

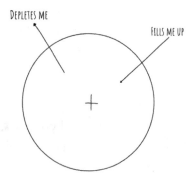

OBJECTIVE: Communication

SUGGESTED DURATION: 1 hour

PHYSICAL AND ONLINE ENVIRONMENTS

CAN BE PLAYED ASYNCHRONOUSLY

FRAME: Group Focus

In the Before Times, when gatherings happened most often in a shared physical space, the space itself ensured a certain amount of focus by a group, the way a frame keeps the focus on the painting inside it. The constraint literally kept bodies from wandering, and that meant minds were on a short leash, too.

With online meetings, the space a person has around them, the distractions within that space, and the fact that people are geographically dispersed, can make it a challenge. Toss in half a dozen "You're on mute!" alerts, a full group conversation in the chat window, a couple of private conversations in that same window, including one that someone accidentally makes public, two or three slow feeds in the group, one person who has construction noise in the background, a steady stream of calls, emails and texts flying at every person in the group for the duration, along with three or four social media feeds that need tending...pretty soon you've got a zombie movie on your hands. You're a character in *The Zooming Dead*. Here's an exercise to help you sharpen a group's focus on days when people are dulled and distracted by their local circumstances.

GAME: Online Mirroring

Ask everyone to put their online display on gallery view so they can see everyone on the screen, not only the current speaker. Up to 20 people can play. Everyone in the gallery must be visible on *one screen*.

- In Part One of the game, a host/facilitator or a person they designate begins by making a gesture that everyone in the group mirrors. The leader's movements are to be within the video frame and made in such a way that everyone can see and follow along. Simple gestures work best. Scratching one's nose, fluttering hands, tugging an earlobe. The focus is on getting the entire group moving in unison, segueing smoothly from one gesture to the next. If possible, do not use virtual backgrounds–they make movements hard to track.

- In Part Two, the leader (the person the group is mirroring) calls out the name of someone else in the group to lead the action. After leading for 10-20 seconds, that person names the next person to lead the action, and so on. (Alternatively, a host/facilitator can call out the names). The focus in this part of the game is on making smooth transitions in leadership from one person to the next without breaking the tempo and momentum of the activity. This activity continues until the group experiences a flow state, with the leaders changing at random intervals and the group transitioning smoothly with no 'stoppage of play.'

- Next, the group debriefs. What did people notice? What made gestures easier or more difficult to follow?

Were transitions in leadership clean, or were they confusing? Why? If tempo and momentum were lost, what were the causes? How do these observations relate to the group's current communication and collaboration practices? Using this same analogy, what adjustments might be made in the group's current practices to improve them?

- Part Three of the game is optional. The facilitator asks for a volunteer and assigns that person to a waiting room. When the person leaves, the host/facilitator assigns someone in the group to lead the mirroring activity, as in Part One. As soon as the group's mirroring is in sync, the host/facilitator brings the person in the waiting room back into the full group, at which point their objective is to *identify the person leading the activity.* Conversely, the group's focus is on *hiding the identity of the person leading the activity.* This activity can be repeated, with different people sent to the waiting room.

- A debrief at the end of the game puts the group's performance on the hot spot. What kept the guesser guessing, or made it easier for them to spot the leader? How visible is an ideal leader? How can leadership be shared? What is the 'invisible work' that contributes to effective leadership?

OBJECTIVE: Collaboration, Communication

SUGGESTED DURATION: 30 mins

ONLINE ENVIRONMENTS

FRAME: Improving Environment

Sometimes all it takes is a small adjustment in a group's process to affect the types of outcomes that process yields. When you feel your outcomes have become static, stale or predictable—and what you want outcomes that are dynamic, fresh and innovative—you can be better off working at changing the process that produces the outcomes rather than try and wrench the new outcomes out of the same old process. One of the elements of any group's process is its space of collaboration—what we call environment. For example, a circular seating arrangement will be much more dynamic than one where everyone is facing the front of the room, looking at the backs of heads.

GAME: Space Inventors

Here's a game for a group to make minor adjustments to its environment in order to break habits and routines in its work. Think of it as being a chiropractor for the room. Minor adjustments can have major impacts!

- Give each person in your group five sticky notes.

- Have them put sticky notes on anything in the room they would like to see changed. It can be anything from the temperature to the table. Every person must claim a piece of the environment that nobody else has tagged.

- The group then spends three to five minutes (depending on the size of group) riffing on the possible changes that can be made to each item that's tagged. The changes must be realistic and immediate. Items get voted on by the full group so that one change can be made to each tagged object.

- The group will be given five minutes to rearrange the current environment, making the changes recommended by the group.

- If there's a work agenda following the re-arrangement, the group spends five minutes at the end, discussing the differences between the way they conducted business and how it would've been different in the unchanged environment.

- The differences are noted, codified, and shared in a memo to the larger organization so that the micro changes produced by one game of Space Inventors can have a macro impact.

OBJECTIVE: Innovation, Collaboration

SUGGESTED DURATION: 2 hours

PHYSICAL ENVIRONMENTS

FRAME: Managing Change

Most times, what got us here won't get us there. It's important to do unlearning reviews and see what you need to let go of in order to shift and make room for something new. Too often, we see groups strive for something new and creative when eliminating or changing the parts of their process that inhibit creativity. Creativity wants to happen. Is happening. Will happen. Just as long as you don't get in its way. This game will shift your modus operandi from the status quo to novum orbis, and you will not have to be a lawyer or know a word of Ancient Latin to do it. Okay, you will have to know three Ancient Latin phrases. But you don't need a law degree to play. So there's that.

GAME: New Juice

For this game, you will need to know Ancient Latin phrases: *status quo* (a normal situation) and *suci novum* (new juice). This game is about 'juicing' the status quo to shift perspectives and productively evolve a current scenario.

- Grab a piece of paper or a whiteboard and make two columns. Label the left column *Status Quo* and the right column *Suci Novum*.

- Spend five minutes listing basic status quo scenarios from your work and, optionally, your personal life, in the *Status Quo* column. A list might look something like this–

STATUS QUO
I work in training
I'm internally focused
I like to cook
I crunch numbers
I blog
I play tennis
We are a team
I worry a lot

- Now consider what kind of fresh energy, i.e., new juice, you can bring to each of these scenarios. What could it be? What would give you a new way of working, a fresh perspective on your current situation, or might simply make you a better person to be around?

  Spend ten minutes listing your new juice in the *Suci Novum* column to correspond to each *Status Quo* item. Your board might look something like this–

STATUS QUO	SUCI NOVUM
I work in training	Learn something new
I'm internally focused	Talk to our customers
I like to cook	Open a restaurant
I crunch numbers	Crunch something else
I blog	Make a podcast
I play tennis	Get better at serving
We are a team	Better communication
I worry a lot	Don't worry so much

- Okay, we lied. You need to know a third Ancient Latin phrase for this game: *prius haustu*, which means first sip. Add a third column between the other two. Label it, *Prius Haustu*. In this column, list a small first step you can make, a pilot, a trial, i.e., a 'first sip of the new juice.' A board might now look like this–

STATUS QUO	PRIUS HAUSTU	SUCI NOVUM
I work in training	Sign up for beekeeping course	Learn something new
I'm internally focused	Do a call center day	Talk to our customers
I like to cook	Design a menu	Open a restaurant
I crunch numbers	Buy a nutcracker	Crunch something else
I blog	Buy a mic	Make a podcast
I play tennis	Watch YT videos	Get better at serving
We are a team	Host a dinner	Better communication
I worry a lot	Meditate in morning	Don't worry so much

- Now throw away the *Status Quo* and *Suci Novum* lists and keep your *Prius Haustu* list. Set a time limit for each item–how long will you give yourself to take a first sip of your new juice? Allow yourself no more than a week for any item. If you think it will take more than a week to do something, break it down into a smaller sip because you are obviously taking too big of a gulp. In the list above, it would take most managers more than a week to schedule and host a dinner for their team. A gulp! You'll choke! Take a smaller sip. A person might change that item to 'Invite the team to dinner.'

Take your first sips of the new juices to shift each thing on your list, and you will notice how the world around you changes. Savor the changes.

OBJECTIVE: Innovation, Collaboration, Communication

SUGGESTED DURATION: 1 hour

PHYSICAL AND ONLINE ENVIRONMENTS

CAN BE PLAYED ASYNCHRONOUSLY

FRAME: Offsite

We know how off-site gatherings are normally structured. The large room. The breakouts. The scripted agenda. The ranking execs explain the strategy, the direction, the vision, the pressure from the board, the stakeholder stakes. The vertigo-inducing hotel carpet. The boxed lunches with mayo and mustard in packets you can't open without using your teeth. Too much food. The cheap Renoir knockoffs on the walls. The sleep....inducing...after.......noonzzzzzzzzz.

Have we said enough? Get the picture? Let's subvert as many of these cliché as possible. If a typical off-site is a certain type of game, it is within our power to make the adjustments required to design a new kind of game, one where people gather outside the office to discover new connections with one another, fresh energy, and co-create different outcomes that would never happen just sitting inside.

GAME: Wandering Walkabout

This is a game for truth-telling and strategizing that breaks not only with the usual workday routine but with the routines we associate with a typical off-site gathering.

This game requires no technology. No phones. No communication with one's organization for the duration of the gathering. And best of all, no boss! Seems impossible? Do it. Delegate. If you're the executive in charge or the leader of a team, pick someone on the team, explain this game to them, then walk away. Whoever you pick will do a great job taking the lead. You'll be surprised, and maybe a little scared by how well things function without you. In this game, you are giving your team a gift—the gift of your absence.

It's okay. If things can't function without you for a few days, you're not much of a leader to begin with and ought to question how you play your role. Let the group roll up their sleeves while you head for the hills!

Let the group know what time they should meet for the Walkabout, and then turn things over to them.

- Alright, team! Get out that ol' sweet smellin' bug spray and have everyone gather in the lobby in your muck-a-mucks. The group should plan to be gone for two to four hours of ex-plor-a-tion.

  Pro-tip: make sure at least one person in the group has a good sense of direction. You're going to forego maps and GPS and wander by following your group's shared instincts and intuition. Still, you wouldn't want the half-day Walkabout to turn into some type of reality show on the Discovery channel. Take snacks and water if you'll be gone for more than half an hour.

- If you have a destination within walking distance of your office, that's superb; if not, you may need to plan on taking the group somewhere close by. The location for your walk should provide space, either in an urban environment or on a nature trail, for you to walk as a group, within earshot of one another, not single file or separated. Best to select a location ahead of time.

- Choose a theme. This can be one of your company values, or you can take suggestions and choose an idea at the beginning of your walk. As the group starts walking, let the path determine how people interact with one another. If you have people unable to walk, congregate in a park that is easily accessible. Remember, nature nurtures, and wandering keeps you curious, and that's a good thing!

- One or more people on the Walkabout should be designated as List Keepers. The group is to call out to them, and they are to list everything significant they experience on their walk. 'Significance' is *any thought, experience, or observation aligned with the theme the group has chosen.* For example, if the theme is 'Building Tomorrow,' a list made on a nature walk might include seeds, blooming plants, the wind, a baby and her parents, and someone's idea to put solar panels on your company's parking garage.

- The Walkabout can last anywhere from 30 minutes to three hours. Upon returning to your point of origin, the List Keeper(s) will read the items on the list your group has compiled. You will then use each of the items on the list as a metaphor for making a better workplace.

- For example, if 'seeds' are on your list, the extended metaphor might be an improvement in your onboarding process. If someone has an idea to put solar panels on your company's parking garage, remember it's a metaphor. In that case, it might mean enlightening the team with something currently hidden in the shadow or clear up an area where people are currently throwing shade. Spend at least 20 minutes on this part of the game.

- Vote on your three favorite ideas for making a better workplace.

- Make a better workplace.

At some point, you may want to tell your boss what you learned about each other, what you got inspired by, seek support for your three ideas, and why you might want to go on another Walkabout in the future. Or not. Maybe one of your ideas will be to replace your boss. We recommend not sharing that idea.

OBJECTIVE: Communication

SUGGESTED DURATION: Half-day

PHYSICAL ENVIRONMENTS

FRAME: One on One

This is a one-on-one encounter. A two-person m***ing. We all know how important it is to build rapport with the people on our team, but many of us dread this type of scenario. Let's face it, sometimes, even making eye contact in these situations can be awkward. And there's always a feeling that the reason for such an encounter is not a good one—it evokes memories of trips to the principal's office, the doctor, or if you're that special kind of employee, an interrogation by Fern Budnick, your company's head of security. Nobody wants a visit from Budnick.

GAME: Personal User Manuals

Every time we buy a new gadget, a board game, or even a new piece of furniture from Ikea, we are given a user manual, so we understand how they work. What if our co-workers came with their own user manuals? Would we understand them and their purpose more clearly? Learn where they're coming from? What languages they speak? Whether any special handling is required? Of course, we would. That's what user manuals are for.

In this game, people design their own user manuals, then engage in a series of one-on-one encounters in which each person references the other's user manual during their interaction.

Every interaction in the game is one-on-one. In the first part of the game, people pair up and help one another design their own user manuals. There is no set of directions or format for a Personal User Manual–people operate as differently as a vacuum cleaner does from a lawnmower, and their user manuals should reflect that.

Manuals should, however, include certain basic types of content that are typical of user instructions: Warranties, Assembly, Power Source, etc.

- Participants are given one hour to complete their User Manuals. They don't have to be fancy instructions, but they should be easy to read and use.

  Each section should have a header and a simple set of instructions or information. They should be written in the third person, as in the following excerpt from a User Manual for Fern Budnick, your company's Director of Security:

  Welcome to Budnick

  XYZ Inc's Director of Security. A dependable protector of our company's property and defender of its integrity.

  About Budnick

  Prior to joining XYZ Budnick was a Navy Seal

  Getting Started With Your New Budnick

  Introduce yourself when you see Budnick or a member of her Security team on campus. If you have a question or concern, you can email Budnick at fernbudnick@xyzcorp.biz.

The Budnick Guarantee

Budnick can be reached 24 hours a day in an emergency.

And so on. User manual lexicon should be familiar to most people, and you can find abundant examples online to help guide you. Make sure all your manuals are legible–you may want to print them out before beginning the next stage of the game because other people will have to read them.

- After the user manuals have been written, everyone in the group pairs up. They exchange user manuals and read through them like a person would for a product they'd just opened.

- Then they take turns asking one another questions about the operating instructions for their 'products.' Imagine you're calling a help desk. You have questions. What are Budnick's working hours? Where is her office? What does Security do in a weather emergency? Does Budnick know anything about cybersecurity? And so on. Be curious, like you would about your new deluxe coffee maker. You really want to know how someone works.

- After ten minutes, people switch partners and hand their user manuals to their new partner. The process repeats. Do this twice more, so that you have switched partners three times. If your time is limited, you can limit the number of times you change partners.

- For the debrief, have everyone recount what types of questions people asked that were not covered in their user manuals. How might this information augment a person's job description? How might it be useful to other employees? How might it be shared outside the group? How might it affect the way a person does their job?

This game takes a stale old format—the trip to the principal's office, the 360 review, the woodshed, the interrogation—and makes it new by changing the game. It's one-on-one but in a larger group. It's a status game, but both people get to be high status. It's a 360 review, but not by one person; the 'rounded' perspective comes from getting feedback from a group of people.

It's probably better than whatever you've been doing.

OBJECTIVE: Collaboration, Communication, Strategy

DURATION: 3 hours

PHYSICAL AND ONLINE ENVIRONMENTS

FRAME: Performance Prep

This gathering is to prepare a group for a performance. A presentation. A pitch. A kickoff. Business is a never-ending theater. Why would we not use some of the same classic techniques employed by thespians to prepare for a performance? A performance that's designed to win over an audience. To build worlds and invite people in. To stir them from their complacency and disrupt their cozy status quo. Here's a technique for getting a team ready for a Really Big Show:

GAME: One Phrase Five Ways

This is a classic technique for actors made popular in Lee Strasberg's Actors' Studio, whose graduates include Marilyn Monroe, Jack Nicholson, and Marlon Brando. It is designed to lift a performance off the script written on the page and into the space of the stage. It produces this effect by having the actor(s) do a scene using only one repeated phrase. This adds a layer of emotion to the performance. Emotions, not the words on a page, are what move an audience. The playwright's words are written as conveyances for a performer's emotions. Let this same technique work for you and your team, to enliven your next performance in front of an audience.

- Have the group form a circle.

- Have one person step into the middle of the circle. The facilitator gives them a commonplace phrase such as "Here are your copies" or "Traffic was terrible today." They are not allowed to change the words of the phrase at all.

- Have that person step to five different people in the circle, and each time they approach someone, they should speak the exact same phrase with a different emotion each time. They can say, "Here are your copies," as if they are shy, antsy, arrogant, bored, in love, tired, paranoid, too casual, fidgety, eager to please, etc. You get the idea. Play with distance (to the person in the circle), eye contact, and vocal tone and volume.

- After everyone has had a turn using different random phrases each time, debrief with a conversation about what is added when words are spoken with emotion. When can words get too emotional? What is the difference between describing emotions ("We are thrilled to announce...") and conveying those same emotions? What might a thrilling or inspiring rendition of "Here are your copies" sound like, and say about a person or a task?

- Next, select phrases from your upcoming presentation and do the same exact exercise.

- Have the group discuss how your message was received. Talk about how words don't have to change in order for the impact of our message to change in a very dramatic way.

No more standing behind the podium! Move and emote! Just because you are choosing an emotion doesn't mean it's not genuine. Use these lessons to give the presentation of a lifetime!

OBJECTIVE: Communication

SUGGESTED DURATION: 1 - 2 hours

PHYSICAL AND ONLINE ENVIRONMENTS

FRAME: Peripheral Vision

Some of the best, most creative ideas come our way when we are doing other things. Percy Spencer was experimenting with electromagnetic waves for the Navy when a melting chocolate bar in his pocket pointed the way to microwave ovens for food preparation. Another Navy engineer, Richard James, was working on a way to keep ships' instruments from getting thrown off balance by the rocking caused by waves when he discovered that one of his experiments had playful outcomes. And the Slinky toy was born. Sherry Schmelzer was simply looking for a way to give her daughter's Crocs more sparkle. From this came Jibbitz, a multi-million-dollar business.

All these creators got sidetracked from their original direction because something surprising happened in the course of their work. It was the surprise that proved most valuable over time. Here's a game for intentionally sidetracking a train of thought or a direction—not to derail the train completely. Your focus isn't to send anyone off the rails; it's to park a certain line of inquiry to the side, so we can see what else might be coming up the line. What kinds of surprises and unexpected outcomes await us when we take turns that aren't on a journey map or that haven't been planned?

GAME: Three Shifts

Each person brings one idea to the game. It can be written and very specific, as in a production plan, or a more general open-ended idea, as with an idea at the beginning of a process. A facilitator can assign the theme or issue the ideas are meant to explore, such as, "Bring an idea for how to hit our sales bonus this quarter," or "Have one idea for how to increase click-throughs to our site."

The facilitator will have made a set of ten directions for presenters, and we have these folded on ten strips of paper in a hat or container so that they can't be read by players.

The ten directions:

- Stand on one foot.
- Turn and face away from the group.
- Look only one person in the eye as you speak.
- Go outside and then run back into the room with your idea as urgent news.
- Pretend that you are five years old.
- Blink uncontrollably.
- Walk around the group in a circle as you speak.
- Sigh with exasperation after everything you say.
- Sell it like a car commercial.
- Over enunciate every word, exaggerating your mouth movement as you speak.

- At any time during a presenter's description of their idea, anyone in the group can sidetrack them with the words made immortal by the comedian Steve Martin: "Excuuuuuuuuse ME!"

- The sidetracked presenter then draws a slip of paper from the hat, and, without sharing the direction with the group, immediately begins following it.

- The presentation of the idea continues in this manner until someone else interrupts with an "Excuuuuuuuuse ME!" after which the presenter draws another slip from the hat and follows the new directions.

- People in the group can also interrupt a presentation with the phrase "That won't work." At that point, a presenter must find a different way of explaining their idea or choose a new direction in their presentation.

- Presentations are limited to three minutes by each presenter, with a maximum of three sidetracks per presentation.

- The group plays the game like this until everyone has presented their idea with sidetracking by the full group.

This is a good way to practice agility. One story or presentation does not fit all scenarios. You'll have to explain your idea in different ways for different audiences. How you explain it to your CEO in an elevator will be different from how you explain it to your mom. Get ready.

Moms ask questions, no one else asks. And so do CEOs.

OBJECTIVE: Innovation, Communication, Strategy

SUGGESTED DURATION: 2 hours

PHYSICAL ENVIRONMENTS

FRAME: Personal Productivity

Do you ever find yourself up to your eyeballs in to-dos? Booked so far in advance that you must take conference calls in a toilet stall? Do you wake up in the middle of the night to write that email that woke you up because you realize you should've written it the day before? Do you have that ridiculously dumb and dangerous and all-too-common habit of texting while driving? We've all been there. We're there now. And we're going to be there tomorrow. It's already on your calendar. You're double-booked and triple parked, and your coffee with four shots of espresso is getting cold on your desk.

Your time is precious, and you need to take things off your plate to be better at all the other things you choose to do. It's time to make a sacrifice. Edit the scene. Chop the suey. Sharpen your scalpel, Doc. We're going to operate.

GAME: To-Don't List

We've all heard of and made To-Do lists, but what if we flipped the traditional practice of To-Do listing on its head and created a To-Don't list?

- Working as a group, grab a piece of paper or a flip chart, and create a Monster To-Do list. It's great to have a visual so you can see just how crazy booked you and your team can get. Pile it on like it's your plate at the all-you-can-eat buffet. Wouldn't want to ignore that one last cheese ball!

Once you've made the biggest, hairiest, all-you-can-eat To-Do list you can imagine, it's time to begin your diet. You are going to have a bunch of dietary restrictions. With each restriction, you will be able to remove items from your Monster To-Do list.

- Make a second list. It's your Monster To-Don't List. Some of To-Don'ts will be one-time-only restrictions, like dropping dessert from a meal. Others will be permanent restrictions, like going gluten-free.

  This list can include things that are a complete waste of time, things that are draining, things that have flopped, things that could end badly, things that other people or teams should be responsible for, etc.

  - An example of a one-time-only restriction might be "No internet."

  - An example of a permanent restriction might be "Late starts."

  - We'll spot you your first restriction. The restriction is *A gigantic waste of everyone's time.*

- Keep going, dieter! Add as many restrictions as you can by listing everything that drives you crazy about your workplace practices and collaborations.

- Finally, go through your Monster To-Do List and strike everything from it that's covered by your

Monster To-Don't List. In the example we use above, you'd strike everything from your To-Do List that you perceive as a gigantic waste of time.

- What remains at the end of the game is your list of True To-Do's. Go do what's on it.

All great art exists within constraints. The ones you give yourself will turn you from a mass producer of busywork into a workplace *artiste*.

OBJECTIVE: Strategy

SUGGESTED DURATION: 30 mins

PHYSICAL AND ONLINE ENVIRONMENTS

FRAME: Positivity

There are days, and there are days. Some days you're up. Some days you're down. Other days you're grooving in the middle on what a pilot would call a 'nominal' flight path. This is a game for days when you and the team are down. Feeling the weight of the world on your shoulders. When every question seems to result in a 'No' or 'Yes, but' response. None of your ideas are flying. You hate your own stuff; no wonder everyone else does, too. And then you get a call from your child's school and–

Can we stop here and just say that self-pity is the most useless of emotions. Sniff. Sniff.

Time for action. If you make positive moves, moves designed to physically and emotionally counteract the drag coefficients that are keeping you from flying, you will experience lift. Think of the structure of this game as the design of your wings. Its purpose is to get you airborne by eliminating or reducing the effect of the stuff that's holding you down.

GAME: Halos and Wings

How many ways can you support/invest in someone's creative concept or proposal and give it wings instead of shooting it down? In 'Halos and Wings,' team members respond by saying what they like about the concept, what benefits they see, and how it will create value. This motivates the submitter of the concept and encourages the group to come up with more positive ideas about making it work. Devil's Advocate roles and Go-to-Hell attitudes are not allowed.

All ideas are collected during the session on flip charts, and in the end, the group will pick the ones which are most promising in the form of Halos and Wings–support and value-adds.

- For Part One, label a flip chart *Wings* and give it two categories: *Create Lift* and *Eliminate Drag*–two elements of good wing design. Your chart will look like this:

WINGS	
Create Lift	Eliminate Drag

- In the Create Lift column, list all the ideas that elevate your product in the eyes of your team and your customers. What makes it work? How is it, marketable? What need does it fill? How will it inspire people to use it?

- In the Eliminate Drag column, list all the ways you can streamline the idea, solve the problems required to implement it, remove the impediments that might get in the way of its success. Once you've completed your Wings list, you'll move onto the second requirement for an angel–a Halo.

- No idea can fly in a vacuum. Part Two of the game is to give your flightworthy concept a Halo, which consists of all the ways you can surround it with support. Who will help you implement it? What solutions and platforms are available to you? Make a second flip chart sheet called *Halo*. Under it, list three categories–*Control Tower, Runway, and Flight*. Your chart will look like this:

HALO		
Control Tower	Runway	Flight

Control Tower ideas will consist of patrons and sponsors to help your concept take off and give it guidance.

Runway ideas will give your idea time and thrust to gather speed and momentum for takeoff.

Flight ideas will be ways to build an audience who will be inspired when your concept takes to the sky.

- Finally, combine the elements on the two flip charts into one chart called *Flight Plan* that will consist of at least two elements from each category you've created. There's also the momentum you'll build with help from others who want to be part of your journey. Your Flight Plan chart will look like this:

FLIGHT PLAN				
Create Lift	Eliminiate Drag	Control Tower	Runway	Flight

This is your design for a project's success–a flight fueled by positivity, problem-solving, pragmatic thinking, and a chassis lifted by the design you've created for it. Good luck, Angels!

OBJECTIVE: Innovation, Collaboration, Communication, Strategy

SUGGESTED DURATION: 2 hours - Half day

PHYSICAL AND ONLINE ENVIRONMENTS

FRAME: Post Mortem

This is a m****ng where you acknowledge the hard work and time spent on an idea that is getting canned. Oftentimes, teams work on an idea or product only to find out the board decided to change directions. This can cause morale to be low, and the team may also resist jumping onto a new project.

This vigil will be about making an homage to what they did and acknowledging that it wasn't a wasted effort.

GAME: Dearly Departed

It's a funeral. Find a quiet space for everyone to gather.

- Dim the lights in the room, close the curtains or shades and play a Gregorian chant, opera, or yoga music. A somber, meditative soundtrack. You can light incense or candles as long as you don't go too pyro on the room and risk setting off the smoke detectors.

- Next, either as a slide show or a wall collage, put up images and names that represent all your recently discarded ideas.

- For each of them, take turns delivering short eulogies for the Dearly Departed. Talk about what you remember fondly of them. The good times you had together and why they will be missed. Even that embarrassing thing that caused them to get trashed. A little levity is always a good thing at a funeral.

- Remember the good stuff you learned from the Dearly Departed that you'll carry with you each day, and on your next adventure. What you'll never forget about them. How they changed your life, the mark they left on your team or company.

- The game ends when any of the participants say "Amen," "Shalom," "Peace out," "Goodbye, you crazy bastard, we'll miss you," or "I'm hungry, let's eat."

This is a ritual you can perform anytime an idea or project into which people have devoted time and effort must be put to sleep. May their memory never fail to inform those they left behind. That's you.

OBJECTIVE: Communication

SUGGESTED DURATION: 30 min-1hour

PHYSICAL AND ONLINE ENVIRONMENTS

FRAME: Presentation Prep

In baseball, the bullpen is where pitchers get ready to pitch. In animal husbandry, it's where the most potent bovines are housed. Either analogy works for this type of get-together. You can treat it as a warm-up for an upcoming performance. Or you can treat it as the place where that beast of an idea of yours can be warmed up, stomping and snorting until it's unleashed on the world to do its thing.

GAME: Pitchback

Get the team together to practice hitting home runs with your messaging and presentations.

- Without announcing the name of the game or providing any instructions, a facilitator playing the role of Umpire in this game selects a Pitcher to come to the front of the room and, in three minutes or less, articulate a product or company message to the rest of the group.

  The rest of the group represents a typical user, customer, or stakeholder audience. These participants are assigned the role of Catchers. They are to listen and take note of key points being made in the Pitcher's pitch as if they have never heard it before.

- When the Pitcher is finished, the Umpire calls up one of the Catchers in the audience. This person is then designated as a Hitter. The Hitter is asked to 'pitch back,' i.e., replay the Pitcher's pitch for the audience without referring to notes.

- Every time the Hitter 'connects,' that is, re-states a point made by the Pitcher, Catchers are to *clap once*. The Umpire keeps score of the number of simultaneous claps. Two or more simultaneous claps are scored as a 'hit.'

- At the end of the Hitter's pitchback, the Umpire asks the audience to name any points made in the Pitcher's original pitch that the Hitter missed. The Umpire scores these as 'strikes.' The total number of strikes is subtracted from the total number of hits to give a Hitter their score.

- Debrief after every Pitcher/Hitter pair of presentations. Talk about what parts of the message stuck and what didn't. Talk about why. Discuss the language that was used, and if the language stayed the same or was changed.

- The game continues until everyone except the Umpire has played all three positions in the game: Pitcher, Hitter, Catcher.

The winning pitch is the one with the highest score awarded a Hitter.

Details are important in this game and can be the difference between a winning and losing pitch.

The winning team can get awarded baseball memorabilia. The game can be adapted for cricket scoring, in which case, give out cricket memorabilia. We do not suggest awarding cricket memorabilia to baseball-oriented groups or vice versa. Stay in your game!

What? You think this game is complicated? Have you ever seen the rules book for baseball? Thick as a brick. And yet a seven-year-old has no trouble learning and playing the game. What are you whining about? There's no whining in *Pitchback*. Only winning!

OBJECTIVE: Communication

DURATION: 2 hours

PHYSICAL AND ONLINE ENVIRONMENTS

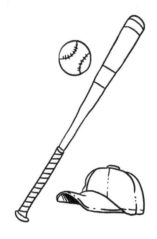

FRAME: Prioritization

A little bit of creativity can go a long way. If an idea is good, it will spin off all the answers to all the problems you're facing. It's relatively easy for creative groups and individuals to sort the good ideas from the bad, or less useful, ones. Often, a bigger challenge for creative people is choosing or prioritizing from amongst many good ideas. When you and I both have strong ideas and the skill and confidence to deliver on them, it can be a recipe for conflict between us. Our brainchildren, after all, are precious to us.

This game gives you and your team a way of prioritizing ideas that's more equitable than a status-based process. It generates more consensus and offers a structured way to merge and hybridize ideas.

The godmother of improv theater in the U.S. and one of our heroes, Viola Spolin, used to distinguish between competition and contest. Competition, she claimed, involves the ego and introduces binaries of winning and losing to which our egos attach themselves. In a competition, according to Spolin, we gain only by winning.

By contrast, Spolin believed that a contest is a good way to extend the capabilities of both groups and individuals. A contest, in the improviser's model, exists primarily for the purpose of getting better individually and together. Winning a contest is a point of focus, not the only desirable outcome of the process.

Here's a contest to extend your capabilities and, at the same time, rally your team behind the ideas they believe in most.

GAME: Tag Team Knockouts

It is not always but sometimes helpful to think of business as a gladiatorial arena where ideas and products battle one another, and things can get bloody in the process. It's no joke. It hurts when people get laid off. Red ink is the color of blood. One thumbs-down from a V.C. emperor and pack your bags.

- This game helps prepare a team for the arena. Good luck to all the gladiators. Also, to the lions.

- In advance, choose three strategic challenges for which your company or community needs 'winning ideas.'

- Use colored tape to mark off an 8' diameter circle on the floor of a room or Coliseum.

- Play the *Rocky* soundtrack as people enter the room.

- The names of all the participants go into a hat.

- A Referee (the facilitator) announces Round One—the first strategic challenge—and ceremoniously draws two names from the hat. The people whose names are drawn step into the ring.

- The Referee rings a bell, and the two people in the ring are given three minutes, total, to each deliver an idea for meeting the strategic challenge. Each contestant is allotted time by the Referee to express their idea. The Referee may also ask questions of either or both contestants and may field questions for either or both contestants from the rest of the group.

- The tempo and tone are lively. Players focus on delivering 'knockout blows' on behalf of their ideas.

- When three minutes are up, the Referee rings the bell and asks people outside the ring to vote for a Winner between the two ideas in the ring. In the event of a draw (tie), the Referee can decide, or the players can play a quick game of rock-paper-scissors.

- If an idea is voted a Winner, the person with that idea stays in the ring; the Referee draws a new name from the hat, and the next three-minute round begins.

- The game goes on until there are no more names in the hat, and one person's or the tag team's idea has emerged as the prioritized idea for that strategic challenge, according to criteria established by the Referee.

- At that point, the same multi-round game gets repeated for the second strategic challenge. And again, for the third strategic challenge.

- Until finally, the group has chosen its three optimal approaches to the three strategic challenges.

Of course, a leader, serving as an Emperor, can, during the game or later, overrule an idea a group has voted for in favor of a different one. A single idea or perspective on a challenge will never be the only one, and all groups have incomplete information. What is not known to a group will inevitably affect its future just as known factors do. This game is not designed to produce a single winning idea but, rather, lots of ideas for competing and thriving in the bloody arena.

OBJECTIVE: Innovation

SUGGESTED DURATION: Half-day

PHYSICAL AND ONLINE ENVIRONMENTS

FRAME: Problem Solving

Sometimes great ideas come out of something we view as a terrible idea. As our friend, the animation Director Bill Kroyer [*Ferngully—The Last Rainforest*], likes to say, "Sometimes you find the right direction by going in the wrong direction, and figuring out the right direction is 180 degrees the other way. If you can identify True South, you'll know how to find True North." We find this idea so compelling and helpful to a creative or problem-solving process, we named it after Bill. We call it Kroyering. Go the wrong way to find the right way. That's the focus of this game.

GAME: Sorry, Gong Number

This activity is designed for fast pitches of new ideas. A game where crazy has its day. You can have an audience, which can be great fun because chances are no one will have ever seen this kind of lunacy with a serious business purpose behind it.

And you get to use a gong.

- Have the leader of the gathering go over the problem or pain point everyone will be working to resolve. Give everyone ten minutes to write down the world's worst ideas for resolving the problem.

- Each player will then get 90 seconds to pitch their bad ideas for resolving the problem with tremendous enthusiasm as if they are genius ideas. The audience is encouraged to moan, boo, hiss, and shout "No!" as if the presenter is tossing live spiders at them. At 90 seconds, the leader hits a gong. At the sound of the gong, people applaud, not for the bad ideas, but for relief from them.

- After everyone has pitched their bad ideas, the group votes on the three bad ideas they feel could most likely be salvaged.

- Split the group into three teams that represent each of the final three terrible ideas. They get 20 minutes to salvage the bad idea by re-working it into a viable and awesome idea. Explain how the new idea works, why it's great, and give it a name.

- The groups then take turns presenting their ideas to one another, this time using the gong for positive emphasis, as a type of punctuation, or musical accompaniment.

Pro-tip #1: Before the game begins, the entire group can have a short discussion about factors that hinder their productivity. It will help make their bad ideas even worse.

Pro-tip #2: Give everyone a chance to vote on which idea is the best idea according to the factors the group agreed on. Once everyone has voted, you have a winner!

OBJECTIVE: Communication, Innovation

SUGGESTED DURATION: 2 hours

PHYSICAL AND ONLINE ENVIRONMENTS

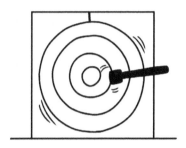

FRAME: Process Analysis

This is a m***ing about m***ings, a way to measure the effectiveness of your gatherings, conclaves, and convocations. How effective are they? What do your people have to say, not about the subject of a powwow, but about the powwow itself? How are they structured and run? How long do they take? What isn't getting done when everyone is called into one? This is a way to turn your team's feelings about how your assemblages are run into data and to examine that data over time as you work to improve your culture and your ROI on 'we time.'

GAME: Acid Test

This game is all about generating data that will help you improve your process, focus, and outcomes for future gatherings. To play the game, you can use either projected screens or poster sheets adhered to the wall. Play the game one screen or sheet at a time. Each screen/ sheet should be divided into five columns, labeled *Metric, Bug, Cost, Fix, Outcome.*

Your sheet will look like this:

Metric	Bug	Cost	Fix	Outcome

To begin:

- In the Metric column, you will have pre-listed the criteria by which you want to assess your organization's m***ing culture. Here are suggestions for the Metric column:

  Attendance. Are people on time? Does everyone attend? Do the people who attend need to be there to solve a problem or address a challenge, or do people attend for political or FOMO reasons? Are roles redundant?

  Environment. Are your gathering spaces suited to their purpose? Sufficient for the number of people who attend? How's the lighting? Does a space invigorate, inspire, confine, or suffocate?

  Structure. What are your rules of order? Are the processes clear? Do people get the agenda ahead of time so they can come prepared? Is the subject of the m***ing connected coherently to a larger organizational agenda or vision?

  Timing. Do invitations arrive early enough? Do you begin and conclude on time? Is there sufficient time allotted? Do your shindigs typically run on too long, like a concert with too many encores? Or get cut short like a rained-out ballgame?

Focus. Do you go over the action items on the agenda or get off track? Do you get to a decision and action items?

Direction. Do people who are running the show keep it moving? Hold the group's attention? Segue smoothly between topics? Resolve conflicts, cluster ideas, honor all voices, and mesh different perspectives into a whole?

Tech. Are gathering places properly equipped? Is the tech checked and working? Can everyone hear a conference call? Is time lost because there are issues with this metric?

• Once all your screens are populated with a Metric, project or post them one at a time, so that your crew of Acid Testers can respond. For each Metric on your list, list one or more Bugs. Bugs are issues that can adversely affect the Metric. What are the problems with your current process? For example:

Metric: Attendance
Bug: People arrive late, causing late starts; poor attendance; too many people attend; wrong people attend; etc.

- Next, for each Bug, estimate the Cost of that Bug. For example, if Late Arrivals is a Bug, estimate the cost, per-gathering, of the late starts. If you estimate your gatherings begin an average of five minutes late, estimate the cost of five minutes of everyone's time who's attending the m***ing, and multiply this recurring Bug on a monthly or annual basis. For example:

  > *Metric:* Attendance
  > *Bug*: Late Arrivals
  > *Cost*: 5 mins x 8 people x 10 m*gs/month = $1800/month x 12 months = $21,600/year

- In the Fix column, list at least one adjustment that can be made to improve the Bug. For example:

  > *Metric*: Attendance
  > *Bug:* Late arrivals
  > *Cost*: $21,600/year
  > *Fix*: Always begin on time, regardless of who's there or late. Create a role of Updater, a person designated to fill in any late-arriving people on what they've missed.

- Finally, for an Outcome, add up the savings that come from eliminating a cost, times the value generated if the saved money is converted from a cost to a revenue-generating activity (for example, if that same amount were spent on marketing and sales).

- Using the example above, If fixing a bug in a team's convening practice results in a $21,600 savings per year to a company, and that company generates $5 in sales for every dollar spent on sales activities, the savings can be converted to incremental revenue of $72,000 a year–just from fixing a tardiness glitch in one team's process.

> *Metric:* Attendance
> *Bug:* Late arrivals
> *Cost:* $21,600
> *Fix:* Begin on time, with an Updater
> *Outcome:* $72,000 additional revenue

- Keep going! Multiply that by all the gatherings that happen with all the teams in your organization in the course of the year. A single bug fix in your convening process can have a fantastic upside. Here's how:

Because games scale, one instance of a game can be faithfully replicated across an organization. Calculate the cost of a single Bug across your organization. Let's say that the bug cited in the example above, Late Arrivals, costs your company $200,000 a year, the total cost of employee time when people are sitting around waiting for gatherings to begin or not at the gatherings on time. If you fix that one Bug, not only will you save $200,000 a year, you will have an opportunity to convert this hidden cost into revenue. If you invest the $200,000 you save into sales activities, and you average a $5 return on every dollar you invest in sales, you're looking at $1,000,000 a year in additional revenue–just by making a game that eliminates wasted time while not penalizing anyone who does arrive late.

Pro-tip: For this to work, your boss has to give up that thing where you are not to begin without them, because the only way they know how to boss is to show up late to everything and have everyone waiting on them like they're a jockey and you're a horse that's not allowed to run without them in the saddle.

Eradicate your bugs. Make more money. Run, horse! Run!

OBJECTIVE: Collaboration, Communication

DURATION: Half-day

PHYSICAL AND ONLINE ENVIRONMENTS

CAN BE PLAYED ASYNCHRONOUSLY

FRAME: Process Improvement

Often, what impedes a collaborative process is a group's inability to acknowledge and reckon with mistakes that have been made. This is a classic fear-driven behavior, and rightfully so—identifying and punishing mistake-makers is an old-school management style.

Evolved managers understand that there are mistakes that call for penalties—those that come about through reckless disregard let's say for the safety of others—and those that could not have been anticipated, did not jeopardize anyone's safety and are therefore learning opportunities. In our experience, most events labeled mistakes are learning opportunities.

This game gives a group a way to greet mistakes made by a team or individual, not with blame, but with gratitude, and apply the learning that comes out of them.

GAME: One Fail, Five Positives

Give everyone a piece of paper.

- Each person in a group writes down something they did at work that was labeled or generally perceived as a 'fail.'

- Circle the fail and draw five stems emanating from the circle. Like this:

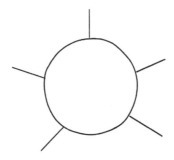

- At the ends of each of the five stems, write down something positive that came out of the fail.

- When everyone in the group has completed their five positives, people will take turns sharing their positives.

- Next, the group tries to identify the one fail from which their positives emanated, followed by a short discussion about what led to the fail in the first place.

- They then spend time reflecting on the overall learning from what might otherwise be perceived as mistakes or failures.

It's nice to know good things can come from our mistakes.

OBJECTIVE: Innovation, Collaboration

SUGGESTED DURATION: 30 mins

PHYSICAL AND ONLINE ENVIRONMENTS

CAN BE PLAYED ASYNCHRONOUSLY

FRAME: Professional Development

There is nothing wrong with wanting to learn new things, but where do we begin? Being a life-long learner doesn't mean that we have all the time in the world. We have more information than we can possibly absorb, and we have more ways to absorb it than we even know where to begin. Podcasts, blog posts, social media, conferences, books, magazines, etc. Whoa, Nelly!

With sources of knowledge so generally available, what's going to gain in value in the future is the ability to bring the right knowledge to the right problem at the right time. What is needed by the learner and when? How does your process also allow for non-linear learning, where what's learned does not have an immediate application? How does it account for emotional learning and the humanities, and result in creativity that can be broadly applied?

This game gives you a way to bring context to your learning.

GAME: Each One Teach One

This classic saying can have profound implications on leadership, collaboration, training, personal and organizational effectiveness. Knowledge never flows in only one direction. It is omni-directional. Here, we give you one way of adding to the knowledge flow. It is far from the only way. Choose your own adventure. Or choose this one. Or, best of all, do both.

- The game begins with the facilitator presenting an Objective for the gathering.

- Everyone will play two roles: Teacher and Learner.

- Each participant spends eight minutes making lists of Stuff You Might Not Know related to the Objective. To use a playful example, if the Objective is to learn about birds, and I am an amateur pilot, I might list similarities between bird design and airplane design. If I'm a movie fan, I might list movies with bird scenes in them. Individual expertise is golden in this game. People should work quickly, listing as much Stuff You Might Not Know as possible in the eight minutes. We are after quantity and flow, not specifics. Not yet.

- At the end of eight minutes, people pair up and decide amongst themselves which of the pair will be a Teacher and which will be a Learner.

- The Teacher reads from their list of Stuff You Might Not Know. If a Learner already knows the item ("Birds have wings, same as planes."), he or she quietly responds, "Knew that," and the Teacher moves to the next item on their list.

- If the Learner learns something, i.e., they did not know the item on the list, ("The bar-tailed godwit can fly for 7,000 miles without stopping.") he or she exclaims loudly enough for the entire group to hear, "I didn't know that!"

- At that point, the paired partners change roles, with the Teacher moving into the Learner role and vice versa. They repeat the process until the Learner exclaims, "I didn't know that!"

When both people in a pair have learned something, the pair splits up and looks for new partners, with whom they repeat the EOTO process, until both have learned something.

Each time a new pair begins, Teachers begin at the tops of their items-worth-knowing lists.

- This continues until everyone in the group has been paired with, and learned something from, everyone else in the game, or for 30 minutes, whichever the facilitator chooses. It will be based on the size of the group. For groups of more than 20, we suggest the time limit.

- The final part of the game is a Summing Up. In this segment, participants share their Learning. The facilitator guides the group in three areas of Summation:

  Patterns - what are some of the patterns in the learning? [breeds of birds, climate-related events, etc.]

Complements - how do the learned items complement one another? [climatology affects migratory patterns, bird breeding habits relate to migration, etc.]

Themes - what are some of the big ideas expressed in the Learning [Climate change affects migration; Those who go and those who stay, etc.]

- The facilitator can query participants about their lists: How far down your list did you have to go before a Learner learned something? How much of your list got used, or did everyone learn the same thing? Are there things that everyone seemed to know? That no one seemed to know? How does our learning connect, and how does it overlap? What are some differences in the dynamics of groups that have lots of common knowledge compared to those who have more connecting knowledge? Why might this difference matter?

This is a fantastic game for the beginning of an initiative. It will show gaps, discourage groupthink, and result in a generous, collaborative, appreciative approach to any project.

OBJECTIVE: Collaboration, Communication

DURATION: Half-day

PHYSICAL AND ONLINE ENVIRONMENTS

FRAME: Ramping Up

This is a get-together where something is begun. A code debug. Due diligence on an investment. A project plan. It's any scenario where you need to walk away with a big picture, lots of new information, a fresh perspective, or a new priority. In this type of get-together, you can collect lots of details without worrying about how they fit together. You can get to know one another and how well your skills mesh. You can identify gaps in a process to optimize that process.

GAME: Quilting Bee

This game honors the process by which a master quilter might approach their work. Quilts are composed in different ways–as stories, repeating patterns, big pictures–but always using panels or squares as the basis of the composition. For this game, we are going to make a quilt with a repeating pattern. Like a master quilter, you will design a pattern using the panels of the quilt as your building blocks.

- Step 1: Using blank white cards or Post-Its, create a 9x9 grid on the wall. There will be 81 empty squares on your wall. This is the frame for your quilt. It will look like this:

- Step 2: For the next 30 minutes, each quilter in the Quilting Bee will make panels for the quilt. Panels are of three different types. Each type should be written on a different color Post-It. Panel types are as follows:

   Type A: On these panels, list *challenges* related to what you're making. You might list items like 'Budget constraints,' 'Time constraints,' 'Competition,' and 'Talent acquisition." List as many challenges as you can in 10 minutes.

   Type B: On these panels, list *capabilities* related to what you're making. If you're a technology company, you might list items like 'Javascript coding,' 'Analytics,' 'Testing,' 'Marketing and Communications,' 'Leadership,' 'Motivated Team,' and 'UX Design.' List as many capabilities as you can in 10 minutes.

   Type C: On these panels, list *opportunities* related to what you're making. On these panels, you might list items like 'Revenue growth,'

'Expand our market,' 'Invigorate our brand,' and 'Complement our existing product line.' List as many opportunities as you can in 10 minutes.

- Step 3: Next, people take turns placing their panels on the quilting frame. The group's focus should be on placing their panels so that they create geometric patterns in the quilt.

The group does not have to use all the items they've listed on their Post-It panels. Their focus is on using color, white space, and geometry to make a pattern for their quilt. This step continues until the group agrees they can all see a completed pattern in the quilt.

Your completed design might have these patterns:

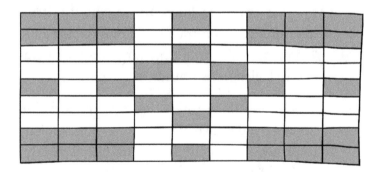

- Step 4: Next, *without changing the pattern*, the facilitator guides the group in moving panels around or replacing them with unused panels so that challenges/capabilities/opportunities are clustered and connected, i.e., every challenge is adjacent to a capability and/or opportunity.

- Step 5: Finally, the group spends the last 45 minutes of the Game documenting the stories in the quilt. The stories are the clusters that best combine challenges/capabilities/opportunities.

For example, your group's stories might be comprised of the five sections blacked-out below:

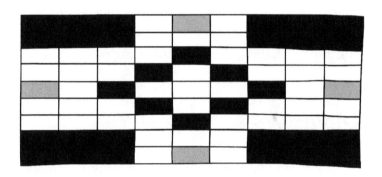

This game can be played multiple times using the same panels to create different patterns and stories.

The focus, in each instance, is on building stories with symmetry and complementary patterns that would be otherwise unseen by the group. You're playing this game to reveal new ways of working together to resolve challenges associated with building something new or resolving wicked problems.

OBJECTIVE: Innovation, Collaboration, Communication, Strategy

DURATION: Half-day

PHYSICAL AND ONLINE ENVIRONMENTS

FRAME: Re-framing a Challenge

Sometimes we get stuck because we are not solving or thinking about the correct challenge, and we could be wandering down a misguided path. One way to combat this is to state whatever problem or challenge we are addressing and then re-express it in another way or with different words. Re-Expression is a simple technique to look at your challenge from multiple angles.

GAME: Re-express Yourself

This is a variation on the old 'Telephone' game. Remember telephones? Us, either. We remember the game, though. Here's our twist:

- Have your group stand in a line side-by-side, with a foot of space between each of you. The game commences when a person at one end of the line *whispers* the 'problem' to the person next to them. Then each person must find a way of re-expressing the problem stated to them, using entirely different language.

  If let's say, the problem is first stated as, "Reduce manufacturing costs," the second person might re-express the problem as "We have to be more efficient," the third person might interpret this statement as, "We have to reduce waste." The entire line of thinking might, therefore, shift from cost-cutting to sustainable business practices, and this will spawn a new set of possible solutions.

- The last person in the line states their Re-Expression aloud to the group. Record the final statement and use it as the basis for a fresh approach to a challenge. This should be fast.

- You can continue to play at intervals in the brainstorm by mixing up the people in the line into a different order or starting the process again using what the last person re-expressed as a new first statement. Or you can begin with an entirely new problem or challenge.

- Game Variation: If your group is larger than ten people, split the group into two lines, and start with the same problem statement.

This game will help a group shake itself free from the way it's currently framing a challenge and generate interesting new approaches.

OBJECTIVE: Innovation, Strategy

SUGGESTED DURATION: 30 mins

PHYSICAL ENVIRONMENTS

FRAME: Re-framing a Challenge

There's a running gag on the old *Rocky and Bullwinkle* cartoon series where Bullwinkle Moose keeps trying to pull a rabbit out of his hat, and instead pulls out all manner of non-rabbits until, finally, he says to Rocky the Flying Squirrel, "I gotta get another hat."

Say you've been trying to pull a rabbit out of your hat for a while now, and the Ol' Bullwinkle isn't working for you. Say you've tried strategies, built prototypes, talked to experts, and have zero rabbits to show for it.

Time for you to get another hat. Here it is. Your rabbit awaits.

GAME: What's Within Reach

We designed this game for online gatherings and play it often with our clients and colleagues. It works to re-frame any subject. The insights a group gets from it are always phenomenal. Here's how it goes:

- Each person in a group takes a turn grabbing any object within arm's reach and describing how it relates to a current project the group is working on or a problem they're trying to resolve. They are not allowed to move out of the camera frame to fetch their object. It's a grab and go kind of game.

- Invite people to be as creative as possible by connecting the meaning, physical attributes, and functionality of their objects to what is currently on their plate for the day or week.

For example:

If their object is a snow globe, a person might describe the difference between the calm of the settled flakes and the chaos of the flakes flying everywhere when the globe is shaken as a way of 'loving the beauty of a problem.'

If their object is a cat, a person might describe the difficulty of getting the attention of a particular executive, and how that person is swayed by good food—so a business lunch might be in order.

If their object is a favorite book, the group might ask them to read a passage and then take turns interpreting the passage considering the current project or problem.

If their object is a dead opossum, maybe you've got a new problem.

This game uses different metaphors to get at different perspectives on a group's work. Each object is like a lens that helps the group see their work in a new way. Debrief the game by noting themes, patterns, analogies, and interesting ideas that come out of the descriptions.

OBJECTIVE: Innovation, Collaboration

SUGGESTED DURATION: 30 mins

ONLINE ENVIRONMENTS

FRAME: Re-Tooling

You're stuck. Stuck. Stuck and out of luck. Stuck like a duck in the muck. Stuck and can't make a buck. Stuck and don't give a ****. You suck. Because you're stuck.

Well...what are you going to do about it? You're going to get unstuck from the muck. Change your luck. Make a buck.

How?

Like this.

GAME: Medium Rare

Most of us have a preferred medium for where and how we write down our ideas, how we capture what comes out of the many conversations we'll have on a typical day. Pen on paper, mobile device, Post-its stuck to every surface in sight, whiteboard, photos, bark at underlings to remember it. You name it. There's no one standard in this regard, and that's an opportunity this game will help you seize.

Maybe the fact that we get stuck in one medium is the reason we get stuck! To change your outcomes, change your medium. To make your idea or story come alive, move your work from a relatively stale technique you use all the time to a new, therefore livelier, medium. Here's a game for that:

- Choose a different medium than the one you currently use. If you typically save in Notes on your phone, try writing with a pen on a legal pad. If you're a big Post-it person (you need to stop that scattered approach anyway), today can be the day you try leaving yourself voice memos on your mobile.

  Bonus points for getting creative with your new medium. When is the last time you wrote with a chunky crayon? Sidewalk chalk? Your non-writing hand? Backward and in a mirror like Da Vinci? Today could be the day!

- Take 45 minutes to write in your rare medium.

  That sidewalk chalk isn't going to write your story on the sidewalk by itself. Shock the neighbors and surprise your children by creating the next passage of your story where the hopscotch used to be.

  What about getting an old magazine and using the words you see on the page and then scribbling over the ones you don't want to use?

  How about refrigerator magnets? Use them to compose a storyboard that you can work into your project, story, or idea.

  Is your vehicle dusty, in need of a wash? Wait! That's not a dirty vehicle. That's a fresh medium! Write the next passage of your project in the dust on your windows before you wash your car. If the spring pollen has settled like a golden worksheet on your vehicle, write in that. That pesky pollen can be your pallet. (Pro tip: Make sure you've taken your Claritin first.)

Are your child's play blocks lying around on the floor? That's your medium for the day. Get to composing! Ask your child for help. Out of the blocks of babes...

- Spend the final 15 minutes of the game converting your rare medium writing into the comfy cozy confines of your standard format. Note differences between what you wrote in the rare medium and how you might have done it in your standard format. Were you more succinct, because sidewalk chalking demanded it? Wordier because your rare medium is voice-to-text?

The new medium may not be scalable. Enterprise sidewalk-chalking may not do much for your valuation. Scalability is not what you're after on a day like today. You want a breakthrough, a pivot out of the doldrums, an inflection point. Moving your thoughts to a new medium will change the way you think, and that's what you want when you're stuck. Like a duck. In the muck.

OBJECTIVE: Innovation, Strategy

SUGGESTED DURATION: 1 hour

PHYSICAL ENVIRONMENTS

CAN BE PLAYED ASYNCHRONOUSLY

FRAME: Retrospective

Back to the Future is such a significant movie for so many people. It blew our collective minds with its existential time-travel tropes, flawless invocations of popular culture, and its creators' (Bob Zemeckis and Robert Gale, guided by their mentor, Steven Spielberg) cliffhanger reminders that many of our futures have been affected by high school dances. Marty McFly has to go back in time to make sure his parents fall in love.

In this frame, we invoke the *Back to the Future* film franchise and play with time travel.

In the original *Back to the Future*, the story takes place primarily in 1955, and 1985 is the present day.

In *Back to the Future II*, the characters time travel to both the Future (2015) and the Past (1955), with 1985 remaining as the Present Day.

In *Back to the Future III*, the action takes place between a present-day 1985, and the year 1885.

The second installment of the franchise envisioned quite a few events and ideas for 2015 that actually came to pass. According to Wikipedia, the following 'predictions' from the film were prescient:

- The rise of ubiquitous cameras
- Use of unmanned flying drones for newsgathering
- Widescreen flat-panel television sets mounted on walls with multiple channel viewing

- Video chat systems
- Hands-free video games
- Talking hologram billboards
- Wearable technology
- Tablet computers with fingerprint scanners
- Head-mounted displays
- Payment on personal portable devices
- Nike's 'Air McFly' shoes aka 'Hyperdunk Supremes'
- A Major League Baseball team in Florida
- Chicago Cubs win the Baseball World Series

Let's imagine a desired future 100 days (can be any duration of time up to one year) from the present day. The objective is to return to the present day with the 'magic elixir' from the future–the actionable insights and directions that will help you realize that future. Or if you're in a crisis management or prevention mode, avoiding an undesirable future fate.

GAME: Back to the Future

This game combines Design Thinking principles with the storyline of the famous movie to produce a solution for achieving a desired future goal or set of outcomes. Ideally both.

The idea of this gathering is to imagine ourselves already having achieved a future milestone with a specific outcome, that you're already 'living' in that world, then work backwards on a timeline from multiple perspectives to figure out how to get back to the present day.

How you'll play it:

- First, break your team into five groups consisting of at least two persons apiece. The five groups are *Martys, Biffs, Lorraines, Georges* and *Docs*. Roles are not gender specific.

- Next, draw a large grid on a whiteboard or multiple poster sheets, with five columns and five rows. The columns represent your timeline, the rows represent your characters' individual storylines.

  Label the far-left column with the Future date at which you want the goal to be achieved. The far-right column represents the Present Day.

  Divide time between Future and Present dates into five equal intervals. For example, if the Future is 100 days from today, the five intervals are 20 days each.

  Label the rows with the names of each character, in this order from top to bottom: Marty, Biff, Lorraine, Doc, George. Your grid will look like this:

	Days 81-100	Days 61-80	Days 41-60	Days 21-40	Days 1-20
Marty					
Biff					
Lorraine					
Doc					
George					

- Prior to playing, the group must agree on two things (or have them pre-defined): a description of a present day scenario, and a description of a desired future (or a scenario to be avoided). In the example used here, it would be a scenario 100 days from today. What does the group want to happen in 100 days? Put these statements on either side of the timeline, like this:

	Future State				Present Condition
	Days 81-100	Days 61-80	Days 41-60	Days 21-40	Days 1-20
Marty					
Biff					
Lorraine					
Doc					
George					

- The focus of the game is to work backwards in intervals of time from the future to arrive at their present day reality. To do this, each of the characters will be constructing his or her own storyline in reverse.

Martys are idea people. In their role, they propose moves the team can make to get back from the future to the present day.

Biffs are devil's advocates, whose role is to shit-talk Marty's ideas, and place roadblocks in the way of a successful return to the present day.

Lorraines represent your customers (or another key stakeholder group), and are responsible for accepting or rejecting ideas proposed by the Martys. They listen to advice from the other characters and create consensus. Their role is to create an optimal path for the group to return to the present day.

Docs are the tech team. They are responsible for the technical specs for the solution co-created by the team. Flux capacitor anyone?

Georges document the steps in 'returning' to the present day. Their role is to make each step clear and shareable.

- The group works backward one interval at a time, with each of them playing their role, i.e. having a say, in each of the intervals, until they arrive back in the present day.

- The facilitator divides the duration of time for groups to work on their assigned areas and then they take turns presenting their characters' storylines to the entire cast.

Time-shifting, as in *Back to the Future,* is a classic narrative device, in which the central characters usually return to the present day transformed in some positive or profound way. This is your team's way of making themselves the main characters in such a story in order to see and experience a current situation in a whole new light.

OBJECTIVE: Innovation, Strategy

SUGGESTED DURATION: Half-day

PHYSICAL AND ONLINE ENVIRONMENTS

FRAME: Retrospective

Once a project is finished, you can't just close shop and head for the hills. Well, we guess you could, but a clean break usually doesn't bode well for the project going forward. A better option is for the team to communicate how they felt about the project and make sure that everyone has a chance to be heard. Retrospectives are a great way to bring closure and awareness to a project. Here's a fun one to get everyone involved.

GAME: Mood-o-Meter

Think of this as like a polygraph for your team's moods over the course of your project. Instead of Lie/Truth, your parameters will be Happy/Sad.

- Draw a graph with a Happy face at the top and a Sad face at the bottom of the vertical axis and your project timeline on the horizontal axis. It will look like this:

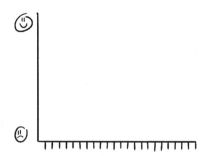

Add as many milestone points on the timeline as needed. Add your sprint, if you're on an Agile team or stop/start if this makes sense.

- Using different colors or styles, have each participant chart their own emotional journey over the life of the project. For less biased input, have each person chart their journey first on a handout, then add it to a master drawing for the full group to view. At that point, your graph might look like this:

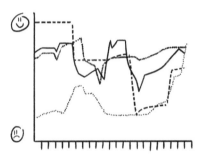

- Have the group discuss why they got up or down at different stages of the project. Note the places where the team's mood was most in sync, and when it was most scattered. Explore reasons why.

The goal of this exercise is to let people remember what happened. It gives them a framing to talk about how they felt and why. Let everyone feel all the feels. Use mood lighting if necessary. And mood rings. And mood food. All the mood modes.

OBJECTIVE: Collaboration, Strategy

SUGGESTED DURATION: 1 hour

PHYSICAL AND ONLINE ENVIRONMENTS

CAN BE PLAYED ASYNCHRONOUSLY

FRAME: Roadmapping

We have a friend who believed he had a great idea for making money. When the geography of Eastern Europe began rearranging itself in the 1980s–with the split of Yugoslavia, Czechoslovakia and the re-unification of Germany–he thought, "There's a killing to be made by investing in a map company. The world will need new maps!" So he invested a ton of money in the Rand McNally Company.

Rand McWho-ly?

Exactly. He made his move at the precise time that maps were turning digital. All those maps, Thomas Guides, and Yellow Pages were rearranging themselves into different forms, too.

That doesn't mean cartography, the craft of mapmaking has gone away. On the contrary, it's just shifted into new forms. We can use cartography to shift the dreary geography of a m****ing into new forms. By playing with cartography, you can see your world in a different frame. You can show the spatial concepts of your work at scale and understand the relationships between people and their roles in a whole new way.

Our friend? Don't worry about him. He re-drew his own map, caught the digital media wave, and made a fortune using new technology as a television producer. It is more important to map your world than to invest in a map of someone else's.

GAME: Mapper's Delight

Early forms of cartography were written on cave walls, and they shifted over time. The purpose has always stayed the same. It is a way to understand or frame the world around us. When your group gets together today, discussions will be led using a map (weather, population. topographic, road, Google etc) as a visual.

- Each person or team creates a map that best represents what they have been working on or an idea that they have.

- Everyone uses their map as a visual for the group to understand their world. Make sure people can understand each other's hemispheres, the equator, true north, and the roadways and rivers that indicate logistics, boundaries, crossings or productive paths. Mountains can indicate obstacles. Operational divisions can be different territories.

- Once you've completed your map, have fun naming the different representations. Make them vivid. That's not just any old 'mountain' to be climbed. That's 'Molehill Mountain,' which isn't nearly as difficult to summit as it might appear. Don't think generic 'river,' think 'Research River' with a 'Database Delta' at its mouth.

- To finish the quest, have everyone see if they can create a large-scale collaborative map that includes input from everyone's map.

"Without geography, you're nowhere!"

— Jimmy Buffett

OBJECTIVE: Innovation, Collaboration, Communication

SUGGESTED DURATION: 1- 2 hours

PHYSICAL AND ONLINE ENVIRONMENTS

CAN BE PLAYED ASYNCHRONOUSLY

FRAME: Social Idea Sharing

Our friend Clint Schaff uses the name 'Campfire' for multi-department gatherings at his company, *The Los Angeles Times*. He understands that many of the ideas and connections that drive an organization happen in social encounters, and informal conversations. Think Slack channels, Facebook groups, private Twitter accounts, elevator, hallway and water cooler chats, lunches—and that classic of the social genre, while waiting for meetings to begin.

Schaff's Campfire concept is designed to bring heat to stories and ideas shared socially by his company's employees that might not find a home in the company's day-to-day operations. It treats cross-functional communication as an opportunity instead of an obstacle. So does this game:

GAME: Light My Fire

This is a way for a group to generate the type of energies we associate with campfires—hot, reflective, radiant, and if-you're-not-careful-with-that-wiener-you'll-burn-it-to-a-crisp.

- Invite people from different departments to gather in a room and sit on the floor in a large circle around four flipcharts at the center of the circle, so that each quadrant of the circle sits facing one of the flipcharts.

- Each of the flipcharts has a different header with a blank list numbered 1 to 10.

  SPARKS is for brand new ideas, or ideas that aren't fully formed

  KILN is for ideas and projects that are on fire, i.e. currently active

  BACKBURNER is your backlog of ideas that got delayed or set aside

  ASHES is for ideas that are defunct or dormant

- The facilitator, playing the role of Firestarter, begins the play by giving each group two minutes to list two ideas that fit the category on the flip chart in front of them.

- The Firestarter rotates the flip charts every two minutes so that each quadrant of the circle gets to review, add to, or amend the lists on the four charts. This continues until all the flipchart lists are filled and all changes complete, or for 30 minutes, whichever comes first.

- The Firestarter then puts all four lists on the wall, and the full group faces them. They spend the next 20 minutes combining at least one element from each list to come up with new ideas that go on a fifth chart labeled FIRES.

- The objective is to have the group agree on three FIRES that effectively blend the skills and priorities of the groups, call on the histories and the futures of their business objectives, and make them the points of focus for the coming day or week.

If you move at a quick tempo, you can play this game twice in an hour. Once is fine, if that's your pace. There is no single pace for productive play.

OBJECTIVE: Innovation, Collaboration, Communication

DURATION: 1 Hour

PHYSICAL AND ONLINE ENVIRONMENTS

FRAME: Stand-up

To help your team make quick, aligned decisions, you can use what we call a Stand Up. You could borrow from comedy and make it about laughing at yourself, your team, or your organization. But such roasting is too rough a road for most folks. Let's leave that type of Stand Up to the Friars Club and borrow from Agile methodology instead. This is the equivalent of an Agile Stand Up. No one sits. Tight structure. 15-minute limit. Fast lists. Fast agreements. Move on. This type of gathering is a great way to begin a workday or a workweek.

GAME: Continue, Consider

This is a framework to focus on behavioral change instead of the traditional 'strength' and 'weakness.' The new approach categorizes feedback as 'continue,' to keep repeating a certain behavior, and 'consider,' to think about changing something. Both approaches come from the world of coaching. Similar to the guidance vs. feedback framework, this distinction helps employees focus on forward-looking, action-oriented changes and casts feedback in a positive light.

- First have one person make a master list of all the items your team has in its current pipeline or agenda. Put each item on a separate Post-It note.

- Next grab a white board or a piece of flipchart paper and create a chart with two columns, like the one below. Place the items from your master list in the appropriate categories. Don't spend a lot of time deliberating. Work toward fast consensus from the group. If there's a tie, or no clear consensus, flip a coin.

Continue	Consider

- The Continue items are those that will get immediate attention. They are, in effect, the day's work. The Consider items are those that will be carried over into future Stand Ups. They are, in effect, your group's backlog.

- Strictly monitor and limit the amount of time spent playing the game. Time permitting, the group can discuss contingencies (e.g. between items) and priorities (e.g. what is at stake for an item) and can adjust the lists accordingly.

This game will add structure to your Agile stand ups, or to any ad hoc hoedown in which fast agreements will help keep things from spiraling into broad and unfocused discussions that aren't relevant to the work at hand.

OBJECTIVE: Innovation, Communication, Strategy

SUGGESTED DURATION: 30 mins

PHYSICAL AND ONLINE ENVIRONMENTS

FRAME: Storytelling

How many times have you and the team worked on a solution to a problem and had to communicate what it was to the rest of the company or to your clients? Does it seem as if you have said the same thing the same way a million times? It's time to stop making copies of yourself and get the team's creative juices flowing. All you have to do is see the signs.

GAME: Sign Safari

- Take your team outside of the conference room and start looking for signs.

- Establish the boundaries of the game. Is it the building you're in? A block or two in any direction? Whatever it is, make sure everyone understands how far they are allowed to go in their quest.

- Each person should bring their phone and have their favorite camera app ready to go.

- Assign the team a time frame of 30 minutes and a goal of returning with six photos of street signs. Challenge them to not only find obvious signs (STOP, ONE WAY, NO PARKING), but also those that are different (NARROW SHOULDER, POTHOLE AHEAD, GATOR CROSSING).

- While the group has been out photographing signs, you have covered the walls of the room with poster paper and laid out marker pens. When the group returns to the original location, have everyone draw the six signs they found on the poster sheets, so that all the signs photographed by the group are visible to everyone.

- Now have the group work on defining the solution they're trying to communicate to their company or clients using the language of the signs as prompts. Where is your solution 'slippery when wet?' Where is there a 'big pothole?' A 'speed limit?'

- Give them 20 minutes to compose a three-minute story using the language from the signs as prompts.

- Now, give them 20 more minutes to make adjustments to the solution in order to improve it. They'll do this by changing, deleting, or adding words to the language from the street signs. For example, YIELD might become YIELD TO CUSTOMERS. A sign that says SCHOOL CROSSING might be altered to COOL CROSSING.

- Now everyone will start getting super creative. You can add or take away letters. What would happen if you added a different shape? See how the signs look different when you really stop to notice them in a different way. Once the group has had a chance to do a few of these, go back to the office and look at your latest ad campaign or product as a team. What words could you add or subtract to change the meaning of your latest marketing pitch, product, or idea? Have everyone "yes, and" one another until everyone is *jammin'*.

OBJECTIVE: Communication, Collaboration

SUGGESTED DURATION: Half-day

PHYSICAL ENVIRONMENTS

FRAME: Team Building

This describes those classic, seemingly useless scenarios, when we sit on the sofa for a long time doing nothing and hardly moving, like reptiles between feeding times at the zoo. This kind of malaise typically sets in when everyone has been working really hard on a project or when you're stalled because of a delay or a problem that isn't seemingly solvable. Maybe it's time to get everyone together for some chuckles and fun.

GAME: Spirit Vegetable

The genesis this game came from a conversation we had about food:

JESSIE: *What is your spirit vegetable?*

MIKE: *Mine is a tomato.*

JESSIE: *Why?*

MIKE: *I am a fruit that everyone thinks is a vegetable.*

JESSIE: *LOL.*

MIKE: *Because I hang out with vegetables and they just assume...but no. Fruit.*

JESSIE: *Nice!*

MIKE: *How about you?*

JESSIE: *Brussel Sprout.*

MIKE: *I love Brussel Sprouts.*

JESSIE: *Surprisingly delicious.*

MIKE: *Ahh...hard to get right, but gotten right, no veg is better*

JESSIE: *At first you aren't sure what to think and then you want seconds...*

MIKE: *A blend of crispy and tender.*

JESSIE: *Totally.*

MIKE: *Getting burned isn't the worst fate, because the center will be perfect.*

JESSIE: *Nice!*

MIKE: *Spirit vegetable—sounds like a game.*

JESSIE: *I'm going to spend the rest of my weekend asking people what their spirit vegetable is.*

Because this is an energy-elevating game, it's important to begin at the low end of the energy spectrum, i.e. in the pits of a malaise.

- To begin the game, have people literally veg out. Slouch in their seats. Mumble their conversations. Imagine themselves on their 4th episode of binge-watching a repeat of a season of *The Bachelor*, a show they don't even like that much to begin with. An empty potato chip bag and three empty La Croix cans (tangerine) scattered at their feet. And then, in this lowest of low-batt beginnings, begin raising the energy of the group with this prompt:

- Each person will share with every other person in the room what their spirit vegetable is and why, until everyone has shared their spirit vegetable with every other person in the room. They must really think about the justification for picking their spirit vegetables, and tie it to their own personality, point of view or life's experience.

- After everyone has had a chance to share, have people pair up, and draw and label their partner's spirit vegetable, without naming the person, like this:

- Next, it's time to make a meal composed entirely of your spirit vegetables. Put all the doodled portraits on a wall so everyone can see what's in your team's veggie bin, and then work together to make a menu that uses all the spirit vegetables, until everyone agrees it's a meal they'd eat.

- For the debrief, discuss the combinations (and, possibly, solo dishes) in your team's meal menu. Would those same combinations work in real life? Why or why not?

Special carry-out bonus: Everyone can keep their beautiful veggie portrait when the game is over as a reminder of the good time had by all.

CAVEAT: Please note that this game must never be confused or conflated with the Native American ritual of finding one's *spirit animal*. That is a sacred Shamanic practice that involves the divination and exploration of the Upper and Lower Worlds to guide one's existence on this plane, the Middle World. It must never be appropriated or taken casually.

Our silly little game is simply about convening in a different way.

OBJECTIVE: Collaboration, Communication

SUGGESTED DURATION: 30 mins

PHYSICAL ENVIRONMENTS

FRAME: Trust Building

Sometimes secrecy is important. When ideas are still in their infancy, call it the concept stage, and subject to lots of misinterpretations, it can be best to let them germinate in the dark. When you're planning a celebration, developing a disruptive product, or mapping a pivot that hasn't been announced, you'll be in stealth mode. Here's a stealthy game.

GAME: Hide in Plain Sight

Shhh. You didn't get this from us, but here it is.

- To get started, identify a space where your group can gather without anyone knowing for sure you're holding a m***ing. A lobby. A coffee shop. The company commissary.

- Don't assemble all at once. Give people a five-minute window within which they are to arrive, and have them arrive at intervals. Don't look suspicious! No wigs, fake glasses or moustaches. They're giveaways. Act normal. Breathe slowly. Don't. Be. Obvious. You want to be seen as a random collection of individuals who happen to be sharing a space.

- If anyone discovers your secret lair and gets nosey, with questions like, "What are all of you doing here together?" look around as if you've been texting with the exterminator about tenting your house, and ask, in your most innocent voice, "Who are you talking about? I'm on the phone with the exterminator about tenting my house." Even if you don't have a house.

- At the 30-minute mark, the game disperses the same way it began. Stealthily. Don't leave en masse. Don't say goodbye. Let the person who came last leave first and continue in that order, so that the first person who arrived will be the last to leave. Stay cool as a cucumber. Don't act like it's a group breaking up, act as if you've got somewhere to be, something you just remembered. Is that the exterminator on the phone, and you have a full-blown termite emergency? Damn. Termites SUCK!

A key aspect of this game is avoiding discovery. Hiding creates a type of tension that will fuel your imagination and creativity. The I-don't-want-to-get-caught syndrome and 'playing right under their noses' heightens focus and attentivenes.

For an even stealthier version of this game, combine it with elements of *Two Truths and a Lie* (p. 196), with this variation: Everyone brings a list of *three lies* related to the purpose of the gathering. If anyone not playing the game comes within earshot of the game, the group only makes statements from their lists of lies until the person is gone.

This game isn't for everyone, or every company. If you have the kind of culture that has people dressing up on

Halloween, names conference rooms for movies, uses code names for unreleased projects, or employs the element of surprise in its narrative (Are you hiring?), this is a game for you.

OBJECTIVE: Collaboration, Communication

SUGGESTED DURATION: 1 Hour

PHYSICAL ENVIRONMENTS

FRAME: Trust Building

How many times in our lives have we operated on a false assumption, assumed something was true when it actually was not, or vice versa? How many times have we made erroneous assumptions about a person, and had to apologize? There are costs associated with our misperceptions. This game is about clearing away clouds of misperception that obscure our vision and come at a cost. Get to know the people on your team while deciphering whether they're telling you the truth, or a big ol' lie.

GAME: Two Truths and a Lie

The game can either be played in person, with face-to-face interactions, online using video, or asynchronously using Slack, Twitter or another messaging platform.

- Begin by having every attendee write down two *truths* related to the purpose of your gathering, and one piece of information that is a *lie*. The truths will ideally be known only to the individual listing them and lies should be plausible. Any statement that is possible but is demonstrably not true, such as a commonly held misperception about your product, can, for the purposes of this game, be considered a lie.

- The game play begins with one person in the group reading their three statements. After the three statements have been read, the rest of the group calls out which of the three statements is the lie. If there's no consensus, the facilitator can take a vote before the person reading their list reveals their lie.

- On a whiteboard or shared document, the facilitator lists the individual's Truths and Lies in separate sections.

- During the game, anyone who has not yet shared their three statements and has listed a same or similar truth as the person sharing their statements, calls out "True Believer!" and their truth goes on the board alongside the other that's the same or similar. When their turn comes, a True Believer does not repeat these truths.

- During the game, anyone who has not yet shared their three statements and has listed a same or similar lie as the person sharing their statements, calls out "Lies!" and their lie goes on the board on the board alongside the other that's the same or similar. When their turn comes, a Liar does not repeat these lies.

- This continues, with attendees sharing their lists in turns, until all the Truths and Lies have been shared.

- For the final part of the game, the group turns its full attention to the board of Truths and Lies and notes any patterns they see.

- If all the Truths have been shared before the 30 minutes are up, people should continue building on the inventory they brought to the game.

- The originator of the game, i.e. the person who summons people together, is responsible for making a list of all the Truths that get shared during the game, clustering all those that are alike, and arranging them in a sequence to create a product or ideation story. After the game, the ordered sequence of Truths becomes a new Product Story around the purpose of the game, such as a scenario for a product launch.

- The last one to arrive has to capture all of the Lies. After *Hide and Go Geek* is over, the person who captured all the lies will create a shared document, and everyone will get to vote on their top three 'Lies That Surprise,' meaning those Lies they'd most like to come true.

The Lies That Surprise become the product backlog, the focus of future games and gatherings. The rest of the Lies are just for laughs.

OBJECTIVE: Collaboration, Communication

SUGGESTED DURATION: 1 Hour

PHYSICAL AND ONLINE ENVIRONMENTS

FRAME: Unlearning

There are days when too much of our time is spent on illusions. How many times have we taken action based on false assumptions or shared rumors with no basis in fact? Have you ever worked with a leader with unrealistic goals and agendas masked by the thin and sensitive skin of fiction? Let's stop and think about our blind spots and the facts we don't question. What about the habits and routines that have outgrown their usefulness? When we get caught up in these chimerical situations, we are drawing conclusions from illusions.

This is a get-together about dispelling the illusions that can cling to a day and lead us astray. It's brass tack time. Welcome to the Itty Bitty Nitty Gritty Committee! Your mission is to audit and dispel the illusions and unlearn the habits that hinder your progress.

GAME: Fresh Take

Perspective is everything. It is often hard to see things in a new way when we have been doing things one way for so long. Our blinders have us making all sorts of assumptions. It is time for fresh eyes. Fresh ears. Today's the day you see things more clearly and hear fresh voices expressing new ideas.

- Gather your team in a room in physical space or

online. Start with a problem or challenge currently shared by the group A process that's bogged down. A project that isn't going as planned. A source of recurring conflict.

- Next, list everything that is *assumed* about the problem situation. For example: It will stay on budget. It will get delivered on schedule. The current team will not change. You will not get sued by a competitor looking to cause you trouble. Roles will stay the same. Etc. In other words, everything people in your group *believe*, but that hasn't yet happened.

- Spend up to half an hour on your list-making, until the group develops an agreed-to list of all its assumptions about the problem situation. Use a show of hands if there's any disagreement about what should go on the list. Don't spend time discussing the merits—you're going to get to that soon enough. Just vote.

- Then make a copy of the shared list of assumptions for everyone in the group.

- From that point on, each member of the group goes through their normal working day, looking to either *validate* or *invalidate* the assumptions on the list. The focus is not on interrogation, but on *listening*.

- Make a point of engaging others—people outside the team in different departments—in the problem, in order to test the assumptions associated with it. The less experience others have with a problem scenario, the better.

- At the end of the day, reconvene your team for one hour. Individuals spend the first 15 minutes scoring all the assumptions on their lists according to what they've heard during their day of 'assumption auditing.' Rate each assumption on a scale of 1 to 5 with 1 being Delusional, and 5 being Valid.

- Total and average the cumulative scores of the group for each assumption on the list.

- Spend the last 30 minutes of the session discussing adjustments that can be made to the problem scenario in order to dispel the five most Delusional assumptions.

Make adjustments based on your de-illusioning game and get more realistic beginning the next day. You'll be satisfied and gratified by how even a small adjustment in your problem-solving can result in remarkably different solutions with better outcomes.

OBJECTIVE: Innovation

SUGGESTED DURATION: 1 Day

PHYSICAL AND ONLINE ENVIRONMENTS

CAN BE PLAYED ASYNCHRONOUSLY

FRAME: Urgency

Too often, we convene our gatherings in a lackadaisical way. We glide into things instead of facing them. We talk around the subject of the moment instead of digging into it and getting the real story. We are non-committal about our involvement instead of taking responsibility. We lack a sense of urgency, preferring to postpone any pain that comes with resolving difficult issues, instead of working through it together, and resolving it in the moment. The people in a newsroom face their stories head-on, and they do it in a way that the majority of their viewers or readers can comprehend. There's an urgency and immediacy to their work. Here's a way for you to bring the focus of a newsroom-in-action to your scenes.

GAME: Headline News

This game is about finding the headline for the work you have accomplished in the past week or on a past project.

- Brief the group on the game, and then have them break out into sub-groups of four or five people each. These sub-groups are Headline News Teams.

- Each group will have 15 minutes to create a Headline News report based on events of the past week. In the breakout sessions, each of the teams will compose a three-minute Headline News report, with each of the team members contributing. They should be encouraged to play with personas from local TV news shows:

As an anchor: "The Mayor of CEOville announced today that new legislation has been ratified by the Town Board of Directors to issue stock grants to all employees."

As a sports report: "Things were looking grim when the Customer Service Bulldogs took the field last week for their tilt against the Chronic Complainers."...

As a weather forecast: "That cold front that settled in when the auditors showed up unexpectedly last week, may finally be behind us, and we can look for warmer days ahead."

As a cooking feature: "Today, I'm going to share with our viewers what happens when you try to make a software souffle."

- Groups return from breakouts and present their three-minute Headline News reports to the full group. When all the groups have presented, the full group votes on segments which would 'go to the Network,' that is, which three minutes, to paraphrase Walter Cronkite, "would be of most interest to most people in the company."

If you want to go all out, have your reporters, in classic TV style, wear something fancy on the top and casual on the bottom. A blazer with tennis shorts. Pearls with yoga pants and flip flops.

FRAME: Visual Thinking

Huddles give teams a chance to identify issues that require the attention of another function or level of the organization. They are short and sweet and a great way to connect before getting into the daily grind. This game brings a visual dimension to huddles that will help you keep them from getting talk-heavy. Adding the visual dimension adds perspective to problem-solving and ideation by unlocking a different part of the brain.

GAME: Huddle Pass

Visual thinking can help trigger and develop ideas that discussion and writing might otherwise leave unturned. Group sketching involves participants building on each other's ideas ("yes, and-ing").

- Each member of your team will get a blank piece of paper and pen.

- They will start by sketching an image related to a concept, idea, or topic they want to explore further and sketch for five minutes. Each pass can last no longer than five minutes.

- Each sketch is then passed to someone else, who sketches another related image on the same piece of paper.

- This is repeated multiple times around the group until the original owners get their sketch returned to them.

- The final images are then reviewed and discussed with the aim of discovering connections that individuals hadn't spotted on their own.

Perspective is everything.

OBJECTIVE: Innovation, Collaboration

SUGGESTED DURATION: 1 Hour

PHYSICAL AND ONLINE ENVIRONMENTS

CAN BE PLAYED ASYNCHRONOUSLY

More Framing

Getting Buy-In

Do we expect for a second that you're going to waltz into work after buying this book and make an announcement to one and all that you've eliminated m***ngs, and what is going to take their place is...*games*?

Do you want us to make the jokes for you?

"So...Monopoly but with real money?"

"You're saying my raise will depend on how good I am at Jenga?"

"Have we been acquired by Nintendo and nobody told me?"

"You mean like...*Hunger Games*? I thought we were already playing."

We strongly suggest not going that route. Just because you believe in the lexicon and processes in our book doesn't mean they'll translate without friction into your workplace. Every change creates friction. Your focus in introducing these changed ways of collaborating should be frictionless intros and segues. Here are a few lubricants:

Begin with your Objective. What do you want to achieve? What is your business focus? Use the five coded areas of focus for each game – Innovation...etc. Communication, Collaboration, Customer Success, Strategy – to connect to your team's/company's business focus.

Use Frames to establish context. The Frames are ways to bring a process upgrade into an already-happening conversation. They use familiar frames of reference for business conversations.

Do not replace the word 'm***ing' with the word 'game.' If you never use the word m***ing again, good for you, but don't be the fool who attempts a transformation in one move. Game is a concept, not a word that'll create clarity about your purpose. Same with gamification. Use this book to improve your collaborations. Do it in your own words. Create your own games or modify these to suit your situation. Remember this is your starter kit.

Our book will help make your workplace more joyful, and your culture more collaborative. These two things are complementary.

Three Scenarios

Owner of a visual effects business:

"The producer called a meeting to see how we were going to cut a hundred thousand dollars out of the post-production budget. When I got to the meeting, there were ten people in the room. The department heads, and a couple of people from the studio. I told the producer, 'Cancel this meeting and the next two. There's your hundred thousand. Problem solved.'"

Agile development trainer:

"I was hired by an auto company to work with twelve leaders of their software development leadership group for two days. These are the people in charge of technology for the entire company, mission critical stuff, and our workshop was supposed to set their agenda for the next couple of years—they call it 'chartering'—and help them settle on the problems that most needed solving. Big problems, crucial to the future of the company and its products. Everyone brought their laptops, and opened them first thing, which is the last thing I want, so my goal is to see if I can make the workshop interesting enough that it gets them to close their laptops. And I'm doing it. Within the first hour, they've all closed their laptops. Then they start getting phone calls and text messages pulling them out into meetings. I don't think after the first hour we had a full group for the entire two days. One manager came in, pulled someone out of the workshop, and they have a two-hour meeting right there in the back of the room while we're trying to do the training! *It was awful. You can't ever get a group on the same page at the same time. I finally*

asked one of them, 'What is the work you're hired to do here?'
He said, 'Develop software.' I asked him how much time he
spends every day, on average, actually doing his job. 'An hour
and a half...I spend the rest of my time in meetings.'"

Sara Goff-Dupont, writing in *Medium* :

"An effective meeting brings a thoughtfully selected group of
people together for a specific purpose, provides a forum for
open discussion, and delivers a tangible result: a decision, a
plan, a list of great ideas to pursue, a shared understanding
of the work ahead. Not only that, but the result is then shared
with others whose work may be affected.»

Game Ode

Fueled by inclusion and co-creation.
There's one for every space and situation
Infinite in variety
Possibility
Malleability
Shareability
Utility
Longevity
Engines of outcomes impossible to predict
From the design of a given encounter
Did the Knickerbocker Rules
Predict Mike Trout or Babe Ruth?
Jackie Robinson? The Field of Dreams? Little League?
That game of catch with my grandpa?
Your bobblehead collection?
Six lines in this poem?
No–
They played their way into being
In playing and seeing
We rise together
As team
As one
From the dugout of our imagination
We take to diamond of a new reality
Spike the soil to unearth
Seeds for new fields
New games
New players

In playing a game
We source rivers of flow and surprise
Give a name to a sunrise
And sing that same sun a song
Like we're putting it to bed
When a day is done
Then do it all over again the next day
With a new *nom de soleil*
And a fresh lullaby
Of a game
We don't ask Why
We just
Play
Until it's time to eat
Then walk away
With smiles intact
Until next time

— Bonifer

About the Authors

Mike Bonifer is a Co-Founder of 21 Day Story, which combines quantum storytelling, Agile design principles and behavioral science in a process for diverse, geographically-dispersed groups to co-create solutions to their biggest challenges.

Mike has devoted a lifetime to developing story platforms and practices. His long associations with the Walt Disney Company, where he was a founding producer of The Disney Channel, and universities such as Notre Dame, NYU, USC and Loyola Marymount, are a testament to his craft.

In addition to *No More Meetings!*, he is the author of five books, including *GameChangers– Improvisation for Business in the Networked World*, and *CTRL Shift*, which he co-wrote with Jessie Shternshus, and several scholarly articles on the craft of storytelling. Mike writes and performs poetry at the historical World Stage in Los Angeles' Leimert Park neighborhood.

Jessie Shternshus started The Improv Effect in 2007 to help people and companies reach their full potential by escaping conformity and adapting to our ever-changing environment using applied improvisation, design thinking and visual thinking.

She has been a key player in internal training and transformations for global companies and organizations such as Tyson Foods, The United Nations, PGATour, Mayo Clinic, Transferwise, Macy's, Johnson & Johnson, Getty Images, Ocean Spray, CapitalOne, Crayola and many more.

She is co-author, with Mike Bonifer, of *CTRLShift: 50 Games for 50 ****ing Days Like Today*.

Jessie thanks her longtime friend Sarah for support throughout writing the book. To her family for creative and moral support to help her see it through and for even trying some of the games with her. A special thanks to her daughter, Maya Shternshus, for helping bring the book's illustrations to life.

9 781946 637154